The Joseph Anointing
"Transforming Jacob to Israel in You"

Victoria Mwango Scott

TABLE OF CONTENTS

Dedication

This book is dedicated to my Grandfather, Jameson M. Chapoloko, my father, Ronald K.C. Chapoloko Sr. and my loving husband, Will Scott Jr. who are my heroes and spoke/speak life and power over me. I am who I am, because of who these men are to me. They celebrated the real me.

My Acknowledgements

To my loving husband Will, who has always believed in me and encouraged me to be me. I love you and appreciate you, more than I can ever fully express. Thank you for being my sounding board with all my thoughts, ideas, flow, and for pushing me to excel when I wanted to give up. You are a wonderful man and you have definitely made this world an amazing one to live in. Thank you for taking care of me and for a wonderful marriage filled with love, adventure, laughs, flowers and coffee.

To my incredible babies Andrew (7), Cassandra (6), and Eric (5), you are the greatest children to me. I couldn't have picked better than you. You make me a better person by how much you teach me daily and allow me to love you. Being your mommy has taught me how to dream God's dreams and reach beyond the stars. Thank you for allowing mommy to write this book and understanding that sometimes I needed to work in silence. You are beautiful, gifted and extraordinary children. I love you, dearly.

To my loving mommy, Evangelist Margaret Chapoloko, you are my rock. Words fail me, sometimes, when I want to express all the gratitude that I have for you. I am here, because of you. How you and daddy (now in glory) sacrificed as parents for as long as I can remember to ensure that we had the best of the best. Thank you so very much. For as long as you live, I will see to it that you want for nothing. I rise up and call you blessed, my Proverbs 31 woman. You have excelled above many and still continue to teach others to walk in like manner. You are one of a kind and I honor and salute you, Woman of substance and virtue. Thank you for teaching me all that I know for always allowing me to be your baby. I can't wait to share your wisdom with the world. I honor you with the deepest respect, from our culture!!!!

To my siblings Veronica Chapoloko (Josh Dorsey), Valerie Smith (Gunnery

Sgt. Julius Smith), and Ronald Chapoloko Jr (Krista Chapoloko). I am so honored that God gave me siblings who also became my best friends. That is favor right there and I don't take it lightly. Thank you for the laughter, the late night talks, the iron sharpening iron moments, and for believing in me even when I didn't. Thank you for always encouraging me to be the best Victoria I was destined to be. I love you forever. Aunty Martha Enga-Enga I love you and appreciate you so much.

To my wonderful in-laws Dad and Momma-Sue Scott, thank you for your love and support, and for your prayers that have carried me through the toughest times. Thank you for being wonderful and more like parents than in-laws. You mean the world to me. To my siblings-in law Jason & Jannie Brown and Kristina Scott, thank you for everything guys: Love you! To the entire Chapoloko, Enga Enga, Nduna, Scott and Smith families, a big THANK YOU for your love and support. Special thanks to Reverends' Cornelius and Margaret Masuwa who have been incredible spiritual siblings to me. Your love and support has been out of this world and a great blessing. One of a kind indeed! There are not enough words to express my gratitude. To my spiritual daughter Mthadanzo Masango, and spiritual son Kalumba Malama thank you for loving me and allowing me to speak into your lives and watch you blossom into incredible pioneers in the kingdom. Thank you Grandpa and Grandma Tisdalle. I love you forever. Thank for speaking into my life and encouraging me to soar.

To my girlfriends… however, through the years have become sisters to me how you've pushed me, when I grew faint, cried and laughed with me and always celebrated me no matter what: To Cheswa Nyirongo, Min. April Little, Min. Ashley Callier, Christina Knight, Benetty Estime, Lucille Swanson, Samantha Findlay, and Raquel Bomberger, Chepchumba Tarus and Chelimo Chamberlain, Kutu Baker, Misozi Houston, Dusu Sidime Bwayla, Kasy Lintini, Dr Bwendo Nduna Chansa and Lydia Asana …THANK YOU THANK YOU THANK YOU.

To my spiritual parents and leaders who have guided, protected, prayed and loved me as their own I love and appreciate you so very dearly: Mom and Dad Fidell (Pastors Samuel & Tracy who are also my incredible God parents), Momma Sylvia Litana Robertson, Pastors Reggie and Juanita Brooks, Pastors Rick and Vera Shymoniak, Pastor & First Lady Leonard Cleckley, Rev. Dwight Banks (who licensed me as minister), Pastor Andrew Thomas (In glory), Mother Alice Smith, Mama Apostle Vanzant Luster, and my precious Uncle Titus and Aunty Edna Kalenga.

Last but not least, Pastors Jesse and Falonda Jones, thank you times a million.

I love you guys for believing in me. To my sisters who added that special ingredient to help me complete this book Prophetess Hilary Butler, Minister Felicia West, Psalmist Jelinda Hill, and Prophetess Catherine Tukes; Prophetess Isabelle Lay thank you for believing in me and helping me soar. Minister Cynthia Carmichael and my dear fiend Katie Spears, thank you for loving on my children (awesome play dates), which helped me finish this book faster. I love you all. Thank you to our friends Pastor Brian and Emily Hennon and the ministries/church families of VCLC, STAM, LGC, NBCA and KDC Church families, Thank you and I love you!!!!! Many thanks to so many whose names I have not mentioned YOU ARE NOT FORGOTTEN. I salute you and honor you, for your love and support.

Foreword

God has truly spoken through Victoria Scott to release a collection of timeless wisdom that will propel you to think, act, speak and live in a whole new way. In a world of constant change, chaos and challenge, people need a word that will give them hope and encouragement. They need a place to anchor themselves and re-gain their footing. Many people are so frustrated in their vision and purpose that they don't realize the enemy's true plan is to distract, infiltrate and destroy.

The Joseph Anointing provides that safety net that so many people are desiring. This Kingdom manual is mandated by God and will shift your whole mindset, concerning the true meaning of purpose. She gives you strategies, formulas and equations that bring you to the brink of true, divine success. This is Kingdom governmental legislation, at its best. You will learn how to decree, apply, create, veto, overturn, build and walk in a place of dominion that you may have never experienced. At the end of the equal sign, you will have accurate answers that apply to your purpose. She is a conduit of God and He uses her as a catalyst of change, in the earth-realm.

Victoria Scott is sensitive to the spirits that have tried to assault and assassinate your God-given purpose. She gives you keys to unlock what truly belongs to you. You will know how to connect the dots that seemed to be missing, with your purpose. There are puzzle pieces that will, all of the sudden, fit perfectly, as you progress forward in God's plan for your life.

This book lets you know that you can win, no matter what you are facing. Worry, doubt, confusion, depression, anger and feelings of condemnation are all attacks on the mind. When someone suffers from negative thoughts, they can take it to heart and lose necessary stamina to walk in their purpose. Victoria Scott desires you to win these all-important battles and embrace the heart of your purpose. She teaches you how to deal with the thousands of thoughts that people think every day and how to focus the mind on the way God thinks of you. There is a tailor-made plan that will fit you like a glove. It will show you how to have staying power!

She assists in the opening of your eyes, heart, mind and spirit to get you back in position to be synchronized with God's power. God's power and your purpose is a winning combination that cannot be refuted! God's DNA is already engrafted in you and you are created to produce. While His thoughts and ways are higher than ours, He still allows us access to the exceeding, abundant place that is assigned to our purpose and passion. He is your Father and is concerned about your Kingdom success. Victoria Scott allows us to know beyond any doubt that God is ready to match and upgrade our investment in His purpose, for our lives. This is not just a must-read, it is a lifetime investment!

Kelly Crews
Kelly Crews Ministries
www.kellycrews.org

Introduction

"And God said unto him, 'Your name is Jacob: your name shall not be called any more Jacob, but Israel shall be your name: and he called his name Israel." (Genesis 35v10)

"All things work for the good for those who love God and the called according to his purpose." (Romans 8v28)

"But let patience have her perfect work, that ye may be perfect and entire, wanting nothing." James 1v4

"What causes quarrels and what causes fights among you? Is it not this that your passions are at war within you?" James 4v1

Israel: one who prevails with God, may God prevail; God preserves.... prevail means "prove more powerful than opposing forces; be victorious."

I am honored to share these insights given to me by the Holy Spirit concerning the life of Joseph, his father, Jacob, and his brothers. I'm in awe of God, for what began as a personal study to gain understanding on something my grandfather shared with me, had emerged into life changing revelations I knew I had to share with the world. These are revelations about the greatness of God through the life of Joseph and how they changed my life for the better. With every revelation I applied, I began to think clearer, to live better, worship deeper and to look at life through a whole new set of lenses. I began to gain a deeper understanding of being a peculiar holy priesthood. I started to experience a whole new level of the freedom Jesus died for and spoke of in John 10:10 (abundant life) and felt like finally exhaling with ease in my core purpose. Naturally, I was compelled to share this wealth of information that I was receiving from Joseph's life with others that were going through life's storms and had questions like I did.

This story is personal for me because of the words my grandfather spoke over me before his passing. He blessed me and said I had the Joseph anointing. Little did I know how his words created an open heaven over me that day! I remember it so clearly, how he asked me to prepare his favorite meal and serve him. I thought grandpa simply wanted a special meal before I left to attend college in the U.S. and that he was going to say a prayer or two over me. I was completely unaware of the greatness of the moment I was experiencing!

It was a beautiful day. The sun was bright and the air crisp. (Sigh) We laughed so hard that day. My sisters and I had a new found love for heels and insisted our tiny framed grandma try them out; of which she was all too happy to try and model. We ate the lunch under the cool shade of the mango tree in front of their house and after our meal we, like every average Zambian family, sipped on piping hot tea with freshly baked bread and scones. Little did I know that what was to happen next would set the course of the path to my destiny. Grandpa called me to his side and began to speak beautiful blessings over my life. They were such powerful words that bring tears to my eyes every time I think on them. Like Isaac, Grandpa, blessed the Jacob in me so God could call forth the Israel in me. He declared God encounters over my life, blessed me as a path maker and a powerful voice in my generation and those to come.

Sadly my grandfather passed away about a year and a half after that; but the words he blessed me with live on this side of eternity reminding me of my destiny and purpose. What happened over the next few years led me to write this book.

The evidence of God's favor on Joseph's life is undoubtedly visible from his amazing dreams to his promotions in Potiphar's house, the dungeon and then eventually governor of all Egypt and savior of his people. As God's favor is evident on the life of Joseph, so will we see the hand of God turning every circumstance in the life of this young man for his good.

This story has taught me in such great depth that no matter how much anyone has messed up, succeeded, triumphed, or failed, etc., if they love God and are called according to HIS purpose, all will be used for the glory of God and their good. I found a new fascination and deeper appreciation for the Lord's sovereignty. That He is all-knowing; aware of every single detail in all creation, past, present, future, and in eternity. I am comforted in this story that God is not side tracked or thrown off by anything we do. Our decisions wise or foolish do not cause Him to stumble, pause nor flinch. He is always AWARE. That does not license us to be careless with our actions, words and character; but rather we should not live in defeat nor condemnation when we do slip and fall. We keep rising and pressing forward towards the mark in Christ Jesus. We will fall and we will mess up, no matter how much we don't want to. Our human frailty guarantees that we will. But thank God for Jesus that does not disqualify us.

As I mentioned earlier, one of the things he shared was that I had the Joseph anointing on my life. I would be a door for my family to be blessed, and what my hand would touch would prosper as it did for Joseph. I am eternally grateful for that word the Lord spoke into me through my grandfather. It has brought a lot of insight, understanding, and peace over the various storms I faced at a young age. It made me rest assured that I had not missed my Kairos moment and not messed up God's plan for my life. You have to understand, to a person who has a mind, personality, and heart of a "cautious-thinker and strategic planner", failure is not an option, neither is there time for plan b. With the patience to think things through tirelessly and play different scenarios in my mind, I always expected impeccable results with everything I laid my hands to. So when things seemed to be going in the opposite direction (little did I know that was a sign that I had heard God), I beat myself up and began to look down on me and my "not-so-major" accomplishments. Insecurities settled in, that I wasn't good enough anymore and I had missed the mark and failed God. Somewhere along the way, I was responsible for this lack of success I had found myself in and I alone was to blame. Oh, BUT GOD! Little did I know that I was exactly where God wanted me to be. I was at the place like Joseph, a servant and slave, so to speak, that he might use that moment to teach me his ways and build his character in me. He wanted to personally teach me and give me a powerful testimony that I could call my own and to be used to glorify his name.

My prayer is that this book encourages you and reminds you of the omniscient nature of God and how He has it all under control as your Father. That no matter what you go through, no matter how devastating or life changing, all will work out for your good if you love God and are called according to His purpose. I pray that this is a tool you use to fight off the voice of the enemy whispering into your ear that you are worthless when you find yourself in the pits and dungeons of life. It is only over when God says it's over. You are not alone when you go through various trials, temptations, and persecutions. Our God has given us a cloud of witnesses and forerunners who have been through the same situations or worse and have seen the salvation of the LORD (Heb. 12v1). May the Spirit of God fill you over and over as you read each page and may he bring healing, peace, and victory to you as seek His face. Continue to run this great race with strength, valor, joy, and power in the Holy Ghost surrounded by the love of the Father and the friendship of Jesus Christ our Lord and brother.

As I wrote this book, I also developed a deeper love for the nation of Israel and this is my prayer and blessings for them: *Father, continue to bless your people. Watch over them, bless them, protect them and may they grow in the knowledge of you and embrace Jesus Christ as Lord. I pray for their protection, peace, joy and your love to fill their land from the mountains to every valley, every spring to fill with water, every table full with rich bread, sickness to leave their land and the glory of God to rest upon them like never before.*

Chapter 1
God's Promise To Abraham

Genesis 12v1-3: *Now the Lord had said unto Abram, Get thee out of thy country and from thy kindred, and from thy father's house, unto a land that I will shew thee. And I will make thee a great nation and I will bless thee and make thy name great; and thou shalt be a blessing: and I will bless them that bless thee and curse him that curseth thee; and in thee shall families of the earth be blessed.*

Years Later

Genesis 15v18: *In the same day the Lord made a covenant with Abraham saying, unto they seed have I given this land, from the river of Egypt unto the great river, the river Euphrates.*

To capture the full essence of Joseph's story it's only fitting to look back into his history. It all began with Abraham, son of Terah descendant of Shem, son of Noah. Understanding Abraham, his great grandfather lays a strong foundation to Joseph's story. Without Abraham there is no Joseph, there is no Israel, and there is no us. With Abraham is where Israel began, so to speak. At the time of his calling Abraham was called Abram (a high father or exalted father) and later God changed it to Abraham (father of many), when he revealed his destiny and calling to him (Genesis 17v5). His name was lined up with his calling, "Father of a multitude or many;" a father to the Hebrew nation and through Christ every gentile [translated into the kingdom of Heaven]. The foundation was laid with Abraham because God made an everlasting covenant with him. Abraham was a descendant of Shem, the firstborn son of Noah. Abraham entered into a covenant with God that he would be the father of many nations and that those nations of the world be blessed through him. God called him out from amongst his brethren and father's household who were still living in a place of transition. His father, Terah, was originally to settle in Canaan but after the death of his son Haran he settled in the town of Haran on the way to Canaan. Perhaps the town reminded him of what he once held dear and had never gotten over losing his son (maybe favorite son). Canaan was the destination for this entire family but Terah chose to remain in Haran. May we never settle for less than God's best for the sake of holding onto what was once dear to us and of what we lost and maybe feel we can never be that happy again. Not to say that losing the child is a small matter to sweep under the rug or treat as a light issue. Terah died in Haran and we find ourselves at Genesis 12 which begins with the Lord calling Abram to leave Haran and continue with the destination of God's promise (the land of Canaan).

When the Terah season of your life is over and your tears have dried, it's time for the Abram in you to arise and take possession of the land, the promises, the destiny, calling, and blessings God has in store for you. Mourn for Haran but don't dwell there; there is much goodness God had for you - so much of abundant life he has with your name on it. Just as Jesus wept with Mary and Martha for the loss of their brother, Lazarus, so does he mourn with you during your Haran loss. Know that the tears are not his hopelessness but his compassion and refers to himself as the Resurrection and the Life. What has died may be resurrected here or in eternity. Whatever he chooses, know that this is for certain He will give you [new] LIFE here and in abundance. Terah was 205 years when he died. Let your mourning days be numbered and for the season they are set for. Let your mourning days/past/history be for a set time, then it's time to move on into the things God has for you. I'm not saying this to cheapen your pain nor neglect your loss. On the contrary, but rather view those as tools the Master can use to bring you further into the things of God. Elisha mourned for the loss of his spiritual father Elijah (2 Kings 2) and after picked up the mantle Elijah left him to operate in his double anointed destiny.

One of the reasons I love the story of Joseph is how evident God's sovereignty is. From hand-picking Abraham in Chapter 15 of Genesis to choosing Joseph in Genesis chapter 40 to be the savior of his people, Israel, we see his omniscience and omnipotence. He chooses whom he pleases because he is GOD and He is LORD over all. When He chose you, He did not make a mistake. You have been intentionally created for a specific purpose. He blesses whom he chooses to bless and calls whom he chooses to call. He had a plan when he chose Abraham and He made a covenant with him. Humans are an expression of the mind of God. When He said 'let us make man in our own image (Gen1v26), He was saying let me duplicate my image or delegate parts of me, of my mind, and express it or clothe it in human form. I am not saying we are God, but rather that we are an expression of his mind that He has manifested. John Maxwell in his book '*21 Irrefutable laws of Leadership,*' states that a good leader duplicates themself. Therefore, God being the ultimate leader, the leader of leaders (better known as the King of Kings), will duplicate himself and have a part of creation made in His image. Because of His loving kindness and favor, He chose humans to carry that blessing. We are the only part of creation after His begotten son to receive such an honor. Love duplicates....

Have you ever found yourself with much to do in a day that you wish you could duplicate yourself to get it all done? God is able to do all things. He is self-sufficient and not in need of any hand to do anything. He is God immortal, the invincible one, all wise God that is self- sustaining and all powerful. He created the heavens and the earth singlehandedly in the counsel of the trinity and effortlessly brought into existence all that we know as life. So why did he duplicate Himself if He can effortlessly handle everything singlehandedly? Because of His incomprehensible LOVE, He chose us and included us in His plans. So He takes His image, His ways, His thoughts, His ideas and places them inside us in the form of His image. Each of us is an expression of the mind of God. This is why in James, the Lord emphasizes that we be careful how we speak of one another for we are made in the image of God. Due to a lack of understanding, we mistreat a person's dream but what that actually is, is mistreating God's dream. It's all about God. It always has been and always will be. When He shows us a vision, it is the Spirit revealing to us the deep thoughts of God towards us. He desires for us His predestined destiny for us. Destiny to bring us that expected end and gladness (Jeremiah 29v11). Because it's all about Him, He will never allow his word to be broken, to fail, to be late nor to lie. He must and will always remain true to Himself even when we fall short and are unfaithful. He forever is faithful (2 Timothy 2v13). When He made covenant with Abram, the fire passed between the cut of the animals and it was a sign that whoever broke the covenant, the same would happen to them. Just like the animals were cut up, God could have fulfilled His promise with direct use of His hand, but He is extremely gracious. He included mankind in His master plan. He included man in His process of greatness and blessed us with dominion, fruitfulness, subduing the earth, replenishing it and multiplication. It is the very mind of God to dominate or have dominion. We are made in His image and have been blessed with the privilege to be such in the earth.

God saw a famine coming in the future and remembered His covenant with Abraham. He could have personally with His own hand prevented the famine from happening with one word or by sending Jesus Christ early to prevent it. He could have summoned His angelic hosts to prevent it, but he graciously involved his people. I believe He does that to show off what He has placed in us. He raised up a Joseph for such a time as that to be used as a conduit of God's glory. I believe God adds a lot of excitement to the story (for us anyways) when He involves us in His great works. It is an honor and a privilege when He delegates to man assignments of power and victory. We don't deserve it, but He is gracious. Think of that the next time you are going through a struggle and God doesn't immediately dispatch His angels to kill the enemy or take you out of bankruptcy or fight in a war. He has chosen to work through you and that is an honor, an exciting honor to be used by God as a conduit for the miraculous, supernatural and extraordinary.

Joseph told his brothers that what they intended for evil, God used for good (Genesis 50v20). It's always about God. Nothing catches Him by surprise, off guard nor stuns Him. Nothing is impossible for Him and any obstacles thrown our way are ingredients for success and exploits. He took an image of Himself that dreams, interprets dreams, loves righteousness, has a great work ethic, forgiveness and placed it in a house and called him Joseph. We should go in to the journey of Joseph's anointing knowing this is all about God and about His faithfulness. Joseph, like Queen Esther, was raised for such a time as that, not to shine as the most powerful man in the world, but to let the faithfulness of God shine through eternity. Do you believe God has raised or will raise you at an opportune time to shine forth His faithfulness and glory both here and in eternity? I 100% believe so. Take this journey with me and let's take a deeper look into the life of this remarkable young man from whose life there is plenty to glean and identify with concerning the journey of dreams fulfillment and destiny.

Chapter 2
Joseph's Dreams
(The Power Of A God-Given Dream)

Genesis 37v1 - *And Jacob dwelt in the land wherein his father was a stranger in the land of Canaan.*

Two generations have passed between Abraham and Joseph. The great Almighty Lord and Creator of the universe had become known to man as the God of Abraham, Isaac and Jacob. He is now known as a God of family, man, households, and generations. Amidst the reality of wrestling God, lying about spouses, sibling rivalry, etc., God has brought success and yielded beauty from the ashes of family chaos.

In Genesis 37v 1, we find ourselves at a place where the waters have settled and now flow at a pace soothing to the ear. In the land of Canaan, Jacob has settled where his father and grandfather were strangers. He had settled in the land of promise. He had arrived and lived in the place God had promised Abraham. The dust of the drama had settled and they have settled in the land that rightfully belonged to them. Joseph is in a family with a rich heritage and history and can be traced all the way back to Noah and even further to Adam.

Canaan has now become home to Jacob, his wives, and children. They are thriving as wealth, love, family, health, etc., is now in their camp and life couldn't be better. At this point all is working for the good of this family. The sun is shining, the bills are paid, and all is well. Or is it? Sadly trouble in paradise is brewing as Joseph has been singled out by his father, Jacob, and is causing his brothers to envy and hate him.

Genesis 37v2: *These are the generations of Jacob: Joseph, being seventeen years old, was feeding the flock with his brethren and the lad was with the sons of Bilhah and with the sons of Zilpah, his father's wives; and Joseph brought unto his father their evil report.*

Genesis 37v3-4: *Now Israel loved Joseph more than all his children, because he was the son of his old age; and he made him a coat of many colors. And when his brethren saw that their father loved him more than all his brethren, they hated him, and could not speak peacefully to him.*

Joseph begins to be singled out at a very young age...this was the kid that in his father's eyes could do no wrong and was the child of his old age. Benjamin was also; so what made Joseph different? It is because he was the first born child from the womb of his favorite wife Rachel, the love of his life. In Jacob's mind, Joseph should have been his oldest child, the beginning of his strength and might, the fruit of a great marriage, blessed by God and of his mother. Joseph's impeccable character further singles out Jacob's love for him. Could it be that because the older you get the more keen one becomes to express how they really feel; that Jacob having this child in his old age had become assertive in expressing his disdain for his ill-mannered older boys? This very well could be the case.

At a young age he is showing responsibility. He's a little rough around the edges, but also still very responsible, as his father put him in management over his brothers' business affairs. In Jacob's mind, it seems Joseph should have been his Reuben and his Judah, the beginning of his strength and his child of promise, where the Messiah would come from. Isn't that like us though? We wholeheartedly believe God will come through in a particular way, through a particular someone, with a particular means but God has a unique way of working unique miracles every single time. Joseph plays a significant role but Judah is who Christ chose to descend from. I will talk about that later in the book.

Jacob's favoritism and God's favor

Jacob's favoritism should not be used synonymously with the love and the favor of God; but we can see some similarities. As a parent, I can't see myself having a favorite child and singling them out by solely spoiling him/her; as my other two watch day in and day out as exclusive attention is being given to one. I love each one; but we have different relationships. Any good parent will tell you the same of their children. As we look closely, we will see that even Jacob's favoritism was used for the glory of God. This is not to condone it, but for us to see that no matter what kind of injustice we face or failures we perform, God is sovereign enough to never let that throw Him off guard. He is well aware of it all. And when we think it's over, He's saying that this is working according to his design. Jacob should not (but he needed to, I'll explain later) have shown favoritism on Joseph because it brought out from his other sons contempt, discord, envy, and malice. They never asked to be born. This was Laban's crookedness at work going on and these children find themselves in the middle of their maternal grandfather's sneaky behavior. Sometimes we find ourselves in like situations, having to deal with issues and problematic traits learned from parents, grandparents and guardians. They messed up and we find ourselves paying for their behavior. If that is you, the story is not over. The Lord will show you through this pages that God will use their mistakes, shortcomings and failures for your good because you love God and are called according to his purpose. In other words, not another day needs to go by that you take a snap shot of your life and make it the big picture. It is not the big picture. It's a snapshot.

As you read what you are going through, it is only a chapter or a couple of chapters of the entire story. Please don't give up. Keep reading and the Holy Spirit will shed light. Listen, their anger towards their brother was a desperate cry for attention from their father. Sometimes people mistreat you, not because of you, but because of the God in, for and working through you. It's got nothing to do with you. It's absolutely imperative to not take some of these attacks personally. God's glory is shining in your life in a unique way and there are people who cannot handle that. We can clearly see that Romans 8v28 is working very powerfully in the life of this family. Every single detail is being used to glorify God and bless this family no matter how evil, or malicious, prideful, or vindictive. I want you to see how incredible God is and can move in your life; no matter how broken or whole it is now. Don't get caught up on the "how" just yet. For now, focus on and rejoice in the knowledge that God is faithful and has the ability to make beauty from ashes.

Looking through our natural eyes, Jacob's favoritism to Joseph is horribly unfair and disturbing, but when we look through spiritual eyes, we see the sovereignty of God in all that. In chapter 4, I will explain how the sons of Jacob represent different parts of us and how, in so many ways, we are Jacob. Joseph represents the dream, the promise, and destiny. There is a God given indicator within alluding to the form of greatness hidden deep in our DNA that we are to decode [with the help of the Holy Spirit]. There is a Joseph in every human being. Actually the structure of Israel (12) is in every man as a gift from God, especially because we are made in the image of God. From a spiritual point of view, Jacob's favoritism was a special type of mentorship. For the next twenty years, Israel would focus on his other sons, but now because Joseph would go ahead of them he needed to carry certain tools and principles with him.

Jacob was speaking life into his future, the future of his children, and the future of Abraham's seed and promise. He mentored it, like Elijah did Elisha, Jesus, His disciples; Paul did for Timothy and so on. Joseph was chosen by God, not himself, to be the dreamer and prognosticated symbol of God's faithfulness for his people. Even his brothers knew that and were jealous of him when he began to dream. Not only was their father showing him special attention, now (we will shortly come to find) even God had started to speak to him selectively and give him incredible dreams. They could not speak peaceably to him because of the rage they really felt towards their father, now embodied as envy of Joseph, and concluded it easier to unleash it on him for receiving the attention. If only they could have seen in the spirit that something bigger was in effect. Jacob was investing into their future. We must speak life into our dreams, and acknowledge them. Keep dreaming and believing in what God has declared and spoken over your life. Don't let anyone, not even yourself, stop you from believing and dreaming because of discouragement, criticism, slander, mockery, scorn, doubt, evil, etc. Your dream is your future no matter how crazy it seems. Remember, it is God-given. The Holy Spirit has ingenious creative ways of showing you what is on the mind of God; for He searches the deep things of God concerning you and knows the thoughts and plans God has for you (1Cor. 2v10; Jer.29v11).

Don't expect everyone around you to understand your dreams, especially since the word says that no eye has seen what God is about to do; but the Holy Spirit is revealing it to you. Think about it. How can they? God was showing Joseph God's purpose for his life and it was his family that despised him. Sound familiar? God gives you an idea and people shun you for it. Think of it this way, your dreams are an alabaster box of worship to God. Only Mary (not even the disciples had received the assignment to pour that oil on Jesus) knew that her purpose was to anoint the feet of Jesus. Imagine if she pulled Peter to the side and discussed her idea with him. He would have probably advised her to do differently.

Alabaster box worship is a very lonely worship. It requires a major shift in one's life style that is very unique and uncommon to others because it's about that individual's exclusive calling and gifts. The moment Joseph mentioned to his father his second dream about the 11 stars, the sun and the moon bowing down to him he began his journey of alabaster box worship. It is the type of worship that is action based that only God can explain. We have no words for it. It's sacrificial worship that is birthed out of a deeply grateful spirit. It looks stupid, and sounds ridiculous. It goes against common sense even to the giants of faith, the 12 disciples, and the Pharisees. To Mary, she was pouring her love on Jesus because her heart, the real alabaster box, was already broken for him and poured on him. So pouring her perfume was an outward expression of what had happened inwardly. Joseph's dreams seemed crazy and so out there; but they had an amazing message. That helped Joseph hold onto God when he was in the pit, a slave in Egypt, and a prisoner in the dungeon. Holding onto a dream is a life-saving act. God giving us dreams and visions keeps us alive and motivated when we really feel like giving up. The reality of Joseph's situation was concrete evidence that presented him the right to think it was over; but his alabaster box worship spoke louder than his trials and thus kept him pressing forward.

No to cliques

When we, therefore, understand that our dreams put us in a lonely category, we must immediately deny all annual memberships and monthly subscriptions to cliques. They are a breeding ground for uniformity and exclusiveness. They don't encourage thinking outside the box and always demand a twisted loyalty. Because of how safe they are (support and uniformity) they attract membership, but leave you at the threshold of mediocrity because cliques don't allow you to be different. Your dreams make you different. That said, when we look at Joseph's ten older brothers, they were a dangerous and malicious clique with one fire to unite their friendship. They envied and despised Joseph. Did Joseph really need to be in the midst of that? Was his favoritism a means God used to set him apart? Was it a means he used to keep the future alive? Your future cannot live with your past in chronological time; they go in opposite directions. Anytime your future and past interact let it be for the sole purpose of the future to appropriately glean wisdom from the past. A lingering union between the two will lead to your stagnation and internal destruction. A lingering union between the two empowers the past to overshadow the future and destroy its potential to birth the vision. Proverbs 29:18a, *"Where there is no vision, the people perish..."*

That meeting place is done in the success of living in the present. There comes a time that your future must be separated from your past in order for you to stay alive and keep pressing forward. Likewise, Joseph had to be separated from his family especially his brothers for a season. He was their future and had to be matured and perfected in the dungeon. Invest today in your future by embracing this:

- the past brings experience
- the present brings action
- the future brings hope

This board meeting of three is designed to help your present-self know what to do today for tomorrow. Knowing how to let your past speak effectively in your life will bring peace in the present. And never forgetting the powerful role the Holy Spirit plays as the greatest influence in your life [greater than your past and future]. In the awesome quote from my brother (Ronald Chapoloko Jr.), he says, *"experience has taught me that the Holy Spirit is the best teacher and not that experience is the best teacher."* The Holy Spirit teaches us how to plan, function, what to learn, and how to road map. Think of it like my family making a trip back to Pennsylvania from Georgia. We can plug our destination into the GPS and the future is set, knowing that it will be a twelve hour drive, give or take, and we will have a an amazing week with family and friends. The past shows us how to pack, what to avoid along the way, how much money to set aside for the trip and what to expect as we travel through different altitudes and states.

This book will give a different perspective to the life of Joseph, illuminating the parallels and will prayerfully accomplish the following: bring clarity to the situations you face and bring answers to the crazy questions that flood your mind, those questions that are maybe too daring to ask because they leave you exposed and vulnerable.

It's easy to look at Joseph's brothers and immediately cast stones at them, for hating their brother. The Holy Spirit has an incredible way of tilting the mirror of his word in my view where I can see myself loud and clear, and conclude with, "I am just like them." God speaks to my future and gives me dreams, insights, plans, mysteries, and my heart and mind rise up to say, "no that can't be right."

- Heart: The Bible says is foolish and has evil motives, intensions, ways—yet we live in a world that strongly encourages us to follow our heart.
- Mind: houses logic, common sense, experience, knowledge (limited but it's there). Paul said that we are to give up vain philosophies or schools or thought. Isn't our mind supposed to be renewed so that the whole body is transformed? It has to think in the realm of the Spirit of God.

Joseph is the promise and his coat of many colors represented his inward array of multi-giftedness. For those who are not familiar with God's deliberate strategy, He put in creation fascinating codes of incredible messages and revelations. In the Hebrew language, you find that letters have numbers and numbers have meaning. The number five for example, is the number of God's grace and anywhere it appears in scripture is related to that meaning. Likewise, colors have meaning too. Joseph's multicolored coat, whatever those colors were, had significant meaning when Jacob purchased or had it made for him; but they also had spiritual significance in terms of what was within Joseph.

Joseph had to start dreaming to be set apart from his brothers because he represented the future and for a while he was going to be developed in the dungeon. He needed the counsel of Jacob to sustain him during the slave times ahead. In the same way, God communes with our spirit daily and in eternity, He talks to our spirits and shares divine mysteries that our minds and hearts don't know about yet but are communicated along the way. Eph.2v6: we sit in heavenly places; Rom. 8v16: Spirit bears witness with our spirit; 1 Cor. 2v9-16: especially 12-14, the human spirit understands the Spirit first not natural man (mind, soul and heart).

v5: *"And Joseph dreamed a dream, he told it his brothers and they hated him yet the more."*

Concerning the obvious revelation of this verse, we must be careful with who we share our dreams with. Not everyone can handle the big dreams God lays on your spirit and heart. Not everyone is happy for you and genuinely wants to celebrate you. For some, it may be that you are more of an asset to them personally than an asset to the kingdom. It's difficult to explain what eyes have not seen or what ears haven't heard nor what minds haven't perceived. You will most definitely sound crazy as I stated in the last chapter. If God has revealed that alabaster box worship to your spirit, how will others understand what has not been revealed to them? Understand that not everyone will be where you are. A lot of their negative criticism will come from minds, eyes and ears that have not been exposed to what you know. Don't hate them, despise or rebuke them, rest in the knowledge that it has not been spiritually revealed to them. If it has, they have not received spiritual understanding. Don't kick yourself for sharing it or hate others for not receiving it. Dreams are exciting, but guard them jealously. Some in their ignorance will trample on it horribly and leave you in a place of doubt and devastation.

This has been written for our learning (1 Corinthians 9v15) so that we don't despise family or those close to us who don't understand or agree with our God-given dream. It's comforting to remember that God's dreams are so out of this world that the human mind cannot contain it except it is revealed and explained by the Holy Spirit. God said in (Isaiah 55v8-9) that His ways are not ours and His thoughts are way higher. Stop trying to convince people about your dreams and start focusing that energy into accomplishing the necessary tasks to achieve your dreams (invest, read, research, plan, learn, etc.) and God will take care of the rest.

For example, a 700 pound individual may not be convincing when he or she expresses their dream to participate in a marathon or the Olympics. He/she opens themselves up to all kinds of scrutiny or advice to keep it safe or disregard the dream altogether. Yet the determined soon-to-be marathon runner runs towards the goal of being 165lbs at the starting line. At that point of being 165lbs, now the critics become supporters because of the evidence before their very eyes. Therefore, keep preparing and get to that starting line, no matter who is or isn't in your corner. You can do this because the most important cheerleader present is the Holy Spirit.

Let's take a different approach to verse 5.

A. I believe Joseph needed to tell his family of his dreams. These were not strangers, outsiders, or neighboring tribes that he shared his dreams with. They were HIS people. HIS FAMILY! The only inner circle he knew. They had the same blood flowing through their veins. They had the same father and the same God. They were the people that should have had his back when the rest of the world didn't. It can easily be taken as foolishness when we look at his decision to open up to them. Don't we do the same thing? There are church members who open up to one another and share their dreams and are hurt by one another. Do we stop going to church because we have been hurt? Obviously, if there is unrepentant sin or physical abuse going on, I do not encourage members to stay and be brought to ruin.

But what is happening here is the very reason why Christians are leaving churches over very small offenses. I wonder if the thought of running away was tempting for Joseph, and whether the love of his father was the reason he stayed because it protected him from his brothers. Assignment lets us know when to go and when to stay. It prevents the offenses from getting in the way of our being assigned to that place to bring healing, restoration, or peace. Circumstances we face create opportunities where running away is much easier than staying. Could it be that maybe forgiveness was already working in this young man? Selah.... what we might see as foolishness, was it forgiveness?

- I may not be getting my way but I'm not leaving.
- Patience is having her perfect work in me right now. What does the Holy Spirit have to say about what I'm facing right now?
- The struggles you endure with those that hurt you the most prepare you for the future assignments that require tough skin. Joseph was able to function as an honorable slave and prisoner in the land of Egypt. He had to overcome many struggles such as having his subjects regard eating a meal with him an abomination because of your nationality (Gen. 43v32).

B. There has to come a point that our dreams are no longer internalized but spoken to begin their journey of fulfillment. I've always found that when I can voice what is in my mind, it brings clarity to what I am thinking and opportunity to clarify the objectives that need to be done. It's the moment where what needs to stay in my head always remains there and what needs to be voiced is voiced. In Deuteronomy 30v19, God commands the children of Israel to speak life and that the heavens and earth will record and align themselves with the words they spoke.

There is power in speaking out a dream; it positions it to take a new level of energy in its journey to destiny. You hearing those words brings on a whole new ball game, and fight in you when you can physically hear your thoughts. As a relational being, verbal communication is vital to emotional health. On numerous occasions, we see an all knowing God engage different ones in the bible to speak their feelings, thoughts, prayers, fears, concerns, joys, dreams, etc.

- Genesis 3 – *Adam, where are you*? This question allowed Adam to observe his surroundings and personally question if he could really hide from God.

- 1 Kings 19: *Elijah why are you here?* Elijah looks at his surroundings and for the first time, we hear him voice his fears, frustrations, fatigue, and hurt. It's in that moment that God visits him in a gentle reassuring way that everything is going to be alright. He provides him with further strategy to keep going, encouragement and direction.

Your mind, heart and soul may call you crazy for dreaming, but keep doing so anyways. This war within our members is a serious one, but can be calmed by the power of the Holy Spirit allowing patience to perfectly work in us. The dream must come to pass because the Joseph anointing is not for Joseph only to be elevated and exalted as an incredible leader, but rather to save the household of Jacob which is becoming the household of Israel. I will go into this more in the coming chapters. Joseph is set in place to fulfill the covenant between God and Abraham. Do you believe that you are called to be a problem solver and an instrument set apart to maintain covenant? That excites me! Keep reading.

Side Note: Jacob rebuked him but observed the saying—Jacob didn't like the sound of it but he didn't ignore it either. You may not agree with everything you hear and see in your God given dream because of its magnitude most of the time, but don't totally disregard the saying. Listen. Listen. Listen. Please be quick to listen. Lock it in the spirit of your mind. This is why when someone prophesies to you, it's usually not strange news, but rather something inside of you has heard this information before. Let the Holy Spirit have his way in your life as he whispers truth and mysteries into your spirit.

Also I don't see a boastful Joseph. Neither do I see a foolish young man when he exposes his heart to his family. When we expose our dreams, we open our heart, and stand in a place of vulnerability hoping that our honesty will create mutual trust. I see his heart desiring new beginnings with his brothers because when he dreamed again he told the second dream to his brothers in the presence of his father. His father being the assuring presence that his heart would be heard and yield positive results. Little did he expect his father to rebuke him too!

Again, remember he's not sharing this with strangers but his family; hoping that if they saw his heart they would see him as an innocent recipient of their father's favoritism. That his prosperity blessing went way beyond their father's granting it, but originated from heaven by the evidence of his dreams. Sometimes what we want is for people to see our heart as trouble-free, with no hidden motives but a heart to serve, a heart to have relationship; a heart that if you look close enough you will see a brother/sister/friend that cares about you. But from that this lesson we learn that sometimes it's not the exposure of our heart that's convincing but the exposure of our fruit. I'll go into more depth later.

Chapter 3
The Pit

Gen. 37v12-14: *And his brethren went to feed their father's flock in Shechem. And Israel said unto Joseph, do not thy brethren feed the flock in Shechem? Come, and I will send thee unto them. And he said to him, here am I. And he said to him, go, I pray thee, see whether it be well with thy brethren, and well with the flocks; and bring me word again. So he sent him out of the valley of Hebron, and he came to Shechem.*

Gen. 37v23-3: *And it came to pass, when Joseph was come unto his brethren, that they stripped Joseph out of his coat, his coat of many colors that was on him; and they took him and cast him into a pit and the pit was empty .There was no water in it. And they sat down to eat bread; and they lifted up their eyes and looked, and, behold a company of Ishmaelites came from Gilead with their camels bearing spices and balm and myrrh going to carry it down to Egypt. And Judah said unto his brethren, what profit is it that we slay our brother and conceal his blood? Come, and let us sell him to the Ishmaelites and let not our hand be upon him, for he is our brother and our flesh and his brethren were content. Then there passed by Midianite merchantmen and they drew and lifted up Joseph out of the pit and sold Joseph to the Ishmaelites for twenty pieces of silver; and they brought Joseph into Egypt. And Reuben returned unto the pit; and, behold, Joseph was not in the pit; and he rent his clothes. And he returned unto his brethren and said, the child is not; and I, whether shall I go? And they took Joseph's coat and killed a kid of the goats, and dipped* *the coat in blood; and they sent the coat of many colors and they brought it to their father and said, this have we found; know now whether it be thy son's coat or no. And he knew it, and said," It is my son's coat; an evil beast hath devoured him; Joseph is without doubt rent in pieces". And Jacob rent his clothes, and put sackcloth upon his loins, and mourned for his son many days. And all his sons and all his daughters rose up to comfort him; but he refused to be comforted and he said, for I will go down unto the grave unto my son mourning. Thus his father wept for him. And the Midianites sold him into Egypt unto Potiphar, an officer of Pharaoh's, and captain of the guard.*

Things were already tense in Jacob's household amongst his sons. The bitterness of their relationship towards Joseph was felt in their cold words that left bone-chilling tension in the air. As much as Jacob wanted Joseph around him the feeling was mutual from Joseph, who was the victim of his brother's jealousy and envy and took every opportunity to not be around them. We now find ourselves watching the brothers in action of what started out as a seed of discord, turning into a murder plot; but eventually sold him and faked his death. The dreamer was gone and now they could have Jacob all to themselves. Would Jacob now love them? Would their greatness be sensed and outwardly celebrated with multicolored coats of their own? Would life now be fair? They thought that until they saw their father mourn for days, refusing to be comforted over the "loss" of Joseph. Their plan had crumbled right before their eyes producing results they never expected. That glow that once covered Jacob was rapidly leaving his face. His smiles now came through tears of hurt and his attention was not always present because somewhere within himself, he was with Joseph.

Joseph's walk to Shechem to find his brothers was to be his last in Canaan for a long time. He was walking into a trap because of walking in obedience. They saw him coming and mocked the calling on his life which they knew was legitimate because they envied him. His obedience to his father walked him into disaster. Sometimes saying yes to God does not land us in the most pleasant of circumstances, but God is still in control. They saw him coming and said amongst themselves *"Behold, this dreamer comes"* Gen. 37v19.

- They were telling the truth, he was a dreamer, but they said it in a derogatory tone. Pay attention to what your haters say about you. It may be said in negativity, but they can see your greatness.

- They hated him for their father's favoritism. How many times, I wonder, do people hate exceptional people because of the gifts God has freely and unapologetically given them? Some examples are administrative skills, business savvy, intelligence, vocal skills, musical skills, impeccable beauty, etc. In other words, people will be quick to discredit others because of their gifts and talents before they express any anger towards God who gave those gifts and talents.

Joseph shared his dreams with his brothers and they enviously mocked him, not only because his dream seemed outrageous, but primarily, it was so grand that it intimidated their mediocrity. Not only had Joseph been favored by their father, but the brilliance of his gifting began to take on a life of its own. He talked differently, walked differently, sounded differently, worked differently and now dreamed differently. He was multi-gifted, talented, beautiful, and clearly showed signs as an uprising force to be reckoned with. When he spoke, he spoke like a learned man, with intelligence, boldness, confidence and one of authority. The distinguished governor ruling in Egypt had started to bloom in Canaan. He was exemplary in character and speech. When he spoke, he spoke out of the excellence of his spirit and that was mistaken for pride because of his brothers' insecurity. Sometimes when you speak it's not that you are prideful, it's that your excellence exposes the mediocrity and insecurity of your audience. When Jesus spoke he spoke with an authority unknown to the masses and was either welcomed or rejected. The ridicule you face is a sheer sign you are speaking from a place of authenticity. Welcome, to Jesus my friend! Joseph in like manner, spoke of destiny, prestige and favor and their jealousy rejected the message of sustenance he brought them. If only they had known that their brother's dreams positively affected theirs, they would have treated him differently. Rejoice when others dream well. Trust me, it affects you too and may even affect your survival.

Gen. 37v20: *Come now therefore, and let us slay him, and cast him into some pit, and we will say some evil beast hath devoured him: and we shall see what will become of his dreams.*

They voiced their plans to destroy his dreams because they understood the power of a dream. They knew them as road maps in destiny. Killing him would surely put an end to his dreams. Speaking to him unkindly (because words have power of life and death) didn't kill his zeal, but made him stronger and bolder. So a physical death would have to suffice. Satan can see your potential and greatness and will stop at nothing to steal, kill, and destroy what God has placed inside of you. The Bible warns us that he will fashion weapons cleverly designed to deter us off our path or put an end to our destiny; but it also says that we are overcomers and those weapons shall not prosper nor triumph over us, even though it looks like they have. That's what happened to Joseph. God sent a Reuben in his life to save him from his brothers' evil attack of death by suggesting they only throw him in a pit to torture and torment him. In the midst of the heat of persecution, the Lord is able to raise for you a safe haven that eases the blows.

Had his brothers known that their actions that day were pushing Joseph into the right direction, they would have insisted to kill him. As well thought out as the devils plans are to trap you and destroy you, they are nowhere in comparison to God's well thought out plans to prosper and deliver you. 1 Cor. 2v7-8: *"But we speak the wisdom of God in a mystery, even the hidden wisdom, which God ordained before the world unto our glory: which none of the princes of this world (demons set over territories, regions, countries, empires and continents) knew; for had they known it, they would not have crucified the Lord of glory."* The enemy always assumes victory, but the outcome is always the same. God always wins. ALWAYS! Check mate. Game over. His main objective, because he is already defeated, is to aggravate God's eye gate by attacking the apple of his eye.

Gen. 37v23-25:
- Joseph came to his brothers.
- He was wearing his coat of many colors.
- They stripped him of his coat.
- They took him and cast him into a pit that was empty and had no water.
- They sat to eat bread while their brother cried in agony. Proverbs 4v17 - *for they eat the bread of wickedness and drink the vine of violence.* Proverbs 9v17b- *bread eaten in secret is delicious.*
- They saw camels coming and Ishmaelites from Gilead with spices, balm and myrrh to take to Egypt.

Joseph embarked on an errand that changed his life forever. Like many other Bible heroes, a simple ordinary assignment or errand propelled them into destiny.
- David takes food to his brothers

- Rebekah waters the camels
- Saul on the road to Damascus to kill more Christians
- Zechariah in the temple doing everyday priestly duties
- The Woman at the well
- Elisha ploughing with his twelve oxen

Little did he know this was no regular errand his father was sending him on! That moment was the last time he'd see his father in 20 years. It was a goodbye indeed. Oh wow, what curve balls life throws us sometimes? When we interact with people, it may be a last encounter with them for a very long time [or the beginning of a season of turnaround and breakthrough!]. It's a beautiful thing that scripture encourages us to be kind and encouraging to one another, esteeming others higher than our selves. We don't know when our last time with people will be.

His father had entrusted him with this important task of overseeing the work of his brothers and returning with a positive or negative report. Have you ever watched a movie secretly hoping it goes a certain way because you know the trouble that's coming? It's like you almost want to tell the character, *"Don't say or do that! It will lead to this or that and I can prevent this from happening."* That's how I felt every time I read this story at this particular point. "No don't go Joseph, you won't see your father and family again. You're about to be thrown into a pit, be sold as a slave by your brothers and live a life as a servant in a foreign land, become a convict and be forgotten. SO STOP JOSEPH." He probably thought the same thing as he sat in the pit stripped of his prestige and class and left under the mercy of his cruel brothers.

God was showing me how much this part of the journey was extremely important to Joseph and to us as we are on this journey of destiny. The pit is just as important as the palace. There are lessons to be learned in the pit that are so important so that we can enjoy the luxuries and the handle responsibilities of the palace. The pit is essential for character building that keeps you strengthened to enjoy the palace. My father always said *"Ability takes you to the top but character keeps you there."* If you find yourself in a pit even though it's painful, this process is necessary and more valuable than you realize. If God allowed it, He will use it for your good (Rom. 8v28). Just let Him show you how. We're going to look at Joseph's time in the pit and see what lessons we can pull from there so we don't feel like life is picking on us or that we must be unlucky. We need to avoid becoming a "why me" type of person.

The stripping of the coat

Joseph's multi-colored coat represented the nature of his inner multi-gifted nature. Although the outer garment could be stripped, ripped, and used as false evidence of his untimely death, the inner garment was God -given and fashioned as incorruptible treasure. Survival in the cold and dark pit and dungeon were dependent on the warmth of the inner garment that clothed his heart, when it seemed that all was lost. His dreams were supernatural evidence of its tangible existence and strength. The enemy wants to destroy what is inside of you and will use the stripping of what is on or of you to achieve that. He doesn't need your car, house, job or accomplishments.

You want your dream and he wants it dead. He wants to kill your hope and discourage your faith which is the foundation of your destiny; and the framework Love attaches to act it out (1 Cor. 13v13). If he can get you to not build a blue print and foundation of your destiny, then love has nothing to act on and build upon. God's love is working through your life. Love always gives and works. If what's inside of you is killed, then the process is delayed or another has to be raised up (Saul and David). We see another outer-garm.ent being destroyed later in the book of Job. His outer glory was destroyed and yet he still held onto God. The Bible says that he never cursed God, nor sinned with his lips, as the devil said he would because his love for God was more than for what God had given him. He had a genuine relationship with the LORD grounded by roots of agape love.

My mother taught us that God uses people to propel us forward and that the enemy uses people to deter us. We see God working through Jacob to speak destiny and life into Joseph's future. It gave him faith to his hope that there was greatness in him and then blessed him with a multi-colored coat. Then, the enemy comes likes a copycat and brings envy and jealousy through Joseph's brothers. Stripping him of his precious coat was a blunt message of their contempt. They thought to themselves, Joseph, you are not as special as you perceived yourself to be. Your dreams will die with you. We want to strip you of your privilege, your smile, the spark in your eye, your poise and your eloquence. We will wipe that smirk of victory off your face every time you get to stay home and we have work in the fields. We want to wipe out your confidence, your worship, your voice, your boldness and your authority.

They come in to send a message that makes him question the great yearning of greatness within him that there is brilliance in his future. Jesus went through the same thing on the road to Calvary. They stripped Him of His clothes and gambled for them, tugged at His beard and put a crown on His head to mock His Kingship and Lordship.

> **Gen. 37v24:** *And they took him and cast him into a pit: and the pit was empty, there was no water in it.*

The waterless pit

Remember, your inner coat of the multi-gifted nature is pit proof. Joseph, being in the pit, did not kill him and it will not and has not killed you either. As excruciating and painful this particular process in the journey might be, please understand that you were built to endure this. There is a lesson in the pit. To be the leader you are destined to become, you cannot avoid the pit. Like the Nile River for Moses, the pit is the safest place to keep you alive and out of the hands of those trying to kill your dream. It's not glamorous, bright, or comfortable but it's SAFE. Its loneliness and increased level of danger keep away your accusers, in this case Joseph's brothers, with a purpose to keep you alive. You are in pain but ALIVE, hurting but ALIVE, rejected but ALIVE, in anguish but ALIVE. Listen, if there is a heartbeat left, there is still hope. It is not the safety of his father's house but he's still ALIVE. You are still ALIVE.

> *Golden Nugget: Rejection is my friend ~ Rejection has taught me so many things that comfort wouldn't teach me. That sin is a heart-hardener. It took them twenty years for the cries of their brother to travel from their ears to their hearts. O God, keep my heart pure and away from sin.*

Joseph, later in the story when he is in the palace, makes an important statement that what his brothers meant for evil, God used for good (Gen. 50v19-20). When you understand the important role your accusing "brothers" played, their future apology will be unnecessary. All along, it was the perfect hand of God doing a transforming work in you. We must be slow to speak before we curse and cast aside key people in our lives that were sent to be sharpening tools for our character building. Jesus blessed Judas and pleaded with him to repent after the betrayal because He understood that Judas was an important piece for His destiny on the cross. Let us hold our peace and speak from a place of discernment when opposition comes our way.

As I stated, the pit was designed to destroy Joseph in every possible manner. Let's take a look at what was happening and what we can learn from Joseph when we are in the pits of our lives.

The pain is very real. Gen. 42v21: "...we saw the anguish of his soul". Anguish is described in the dictionary as "agony, pain, torment, torture, suffering, distress, angst, misery, sorrow, grief, heartache, desolation, despair and dolor. Free dictionary says agonizing physical or mental pain, torment and Merriam-Webster says "extreme pain, distress or anxiety. What this man was experiencing had the ability to let depression control his life requiring years of therapy and prayer to snatch him out of the pit. Faith is not looking at Goliath and saying he doesn't exist. Faith is identifying Goliath and knowing you have God given power to defeat him. Call the pit what it is; EXCRUITIATING and then defeat it. Before we can defeat it, we must first identify it. He was crying out to them with such sorrow and distress to be removed and taken out. Identify with your pain. The path to victory starts with you truthfully voicing the problem and what you are feel. If you are broken, identify that you are. If you are in debt, identify that you are, etc. The pit is a painful place.

It sends a clear message of hatred to all your sense to dull them; but be like an individual with a disability, the survivor in them doesn't allow them to die easily. If anything it heightens the functionality of their other senses to rise above average. Someone who is blind will develop incredible listening skills, listening for the smallest sounds to familiarize themselves with their surroundings. Their sense of smell works at a sharper degree because what their eyes would have told them, their scent will. Likewise, when Joseph's brothers attacked him in their father's house, they attacked his hearing when they spoke cruelly to him. He was still able to feel the warmth of his coat, see his father's love, smell the familiarity of his home and taste the fine breads at Jacob's table. Now everything was stripped from him: no kind words, no warm coat, only darkness in the pit, the stench of betrayal, the cold touch of the earth's dirt, and no bread to fill his belly. The battle went to a whole different level. All his senses were being attacked. No physical factors were there to encourage him to keep his head up. Only God kept him alive.

Psalm 22:7-8: *All they that see me laugh to scorn; they shoot out the lip, they shake the head, saying, "He trusted on the Lord that He would deliver him: let Him deliver him, seeing he delighted in Him"*. If we take David's cry and use it in this situation, we hear this dialogue coming from Joseph's brothers as he is in the waterless pit. "You dare to be different and now look! You rest helpless in the pit of nothingness, all alone and scared. Where is our father now, the father who adores you, and spoils you and cherishes every word you say? Where is he to protect you now? We despise you and we hope you see that. You thought because we are brothers, we'd rejoice in your dreams, but they only made us hate you more."

"It's one thing for our father to love you more and show you favor above us all. It's another thing for you to embrace your greatness and let God shine through you. Why you Joseph? You are favored, beautiful and gifted. Why you? Is it because your mother was Rachel? The woman that dad really wanted? If dad had his way, he, Rachel, Benjamin and you would have been the perfect family. We are here feeling like the extras in the play, just to fill up space in the household. We feel like glorified servants while you and Benjamin enjoy the luxuries of father's table and wisdom of his mind. We would dare not tell you that it is father that we're really mad at because of how he cares for you and pampers you and treats you better than us. No, then you'll see how vulnerable we are and that all we want is to be loved and appreciated. We want our coat of many colors. We want our chance to sit at father's feet and glean from his wisdom and knowledge. Joseph you will die before we ever reveal to you how much we want to be loved; to be you. Because we can't rise to where you are, we cast you down below where we are [into the pit]. (Note: my father taught me "It takes everything for people to rise to where you are and nothing for you to stoop to where they are.") It is as it should be. You are looking up to us now. Let God, who has given you these dreams come and rescue you. Let father who adorns you with coats, come and pull you out of this one. His protection does not reach these borders and we have you where we want you. Let the darkness close in on your dreams and precious visions. Let your bare skin remind you of a coatless warrior. Hear our laughter and know we don't care."

1. The pit is waterless: Some of the toughest times in our lives are in those dry desert-like places where refreshing water is scarce. It can be a lifeless place designed to destroy you. It's a place that is designed to separate you from life. Water is life, especially the word of God. They may have separated him from natural water but only brought him closer to the Living Water that would make him never thirst again (Jn. 4)

2. Saves you from eating idle bread: As Joseph cried out in anguish, his brothers laughed and talked and ate bread. The pit saves you from eating idle bread. Proverbs 17v1 reads, "Better is a dry morsel, and quietness therewith, than a house full of sacrifices with strife." Just like Joseph said yes to his father to be sent to his brothers, we are sent by our father, God, into dangerous territories that seem to strip us of our glorious multi-colored coats. Saying yes to Him sometimes means that we will find ourselves in the pit, a waterless pit, left to suffer and die. When we are sent and have a dream, we must expect to not be popular, be in the minority and not partake in the bread of the masses. Although there is safety in numbers we must understand that there are also times when being alone is just as important. That bread they ate attacked their taste buds and was not good bread. It was bread being enjoyed in the sacrifice with strife or in other words, the bread of evil. Like the Proverbs 31 woman, refuse to eat of such bread. It is idle and futile. There are certain meals you must never partake of. The pit saves you from unfruitful conversations and works that have no purpose but to waste time.

3. Vision vs sight: Sight is what you perceive with your physical eyes and vision is what you perceive with your spirit. The pit helps you begin to test your capability to distinguish the two. What your eyes don't see, your spirit has to so that you can live and not perish. It is a lack of vision that causes us to perish (Proverbs 29v18). Your eyes must go through a season of not seeing anything: not seeing greatness, growth, abundance, support system, success, tangible blessings to test the power of the vision resting in your spirit. The test must happen to prove the authenticity of what God has placed within you. Mourn in the pit, but don't despise it. A deeper level of greatness is being birthed there.

4. The pit reveals who's who in your life: allow people to reveal who they are. You have to know the Reuben in your life and what he represents and stands for. You have to know Simeon, Levi, Judah, Naphtali, Gad, Asher, Issachar, Dan and Zebulun. They are close to you and each represents areas of your life that you have to deal with. I explain that in chapter 4, so stay tuned. At the pit, their true nature is revealed to you. Embrace it, you need it and so do they.

5. The test of faith begins: In the pit, Joseph had to hold onto the only voice he could trust, God's. (Faith comes by hearing the voice of God.) In that

moment, he needed to hold onto God's voice that he was going to live and not die and that, from as far back as his ancestry goes, the faithfulness of God always shines and comes through, no matter how dark the situation.

Gen. 37v25b-28: '*... a company of Ishmaelites came from Gilead with their camels bearing spices and balm and myrrh, going to carry it down to Egypt. And Judah said unto his brethren, "What profit is it if we kill our brother, and conceal his blood? Come let us sell him to the Ishmaelites, and let not our hand be upon him; for he is our brother and our flesh." And his brethren were content. Then, there passed by Midianite merchantmen and they drew and lifted up Joseph out of the pit, and sold Joseph to the Ishmaelites for twenty pieces of silver: and they brought Joseph into Egypt.*'

From the Pit to Slavery

Sitting in the pit probably seemed better than what was about to happen. It went from bad to worse. As if the pit wasn't horrific enough, Joseph was about to enter into a whole new phrase of hatred that would have left him desiring death. His loud cries of anguish dissipated into soft sobs and then into silence allowing him to closely listen to his brothers having a conversation with voices he did not recognize. Were they negotiating? Wait! This was not going to be a session of torture followed by threats to not tell Jacob? Wait! They were selling him into slavery? They were going to separate him from what he loved and called home, from his beloved father and brother? He'd heard of slavery and how demeaning it was. His father treated their servants well and with respect. Slaves were demoralized and treated less than humans. They had no rights and say so. His brothers were selling him and selling him for so little. "Message received guys, loud and clear, 20 pieces of silver, got it" he thought, "You truly hate me."

His brothers didn't realize that when one puts a price on happiness or destiny, they will soon discover what dangerous territory they are flirting with. Certain things must always remain priceless. Even Visa got a hold of that memo! This is a perfect place to interject this thought. No matter how tempting it gets when we find ourselves in pits, don't try to help God because you have caught onto the vision and must find a way to get out and run. Joseph stayed put. It may not look like it, but you are on the path to living your destiny. Jacob's house is comforting, rewarding, motivating and safe, but it's in Pharaoh's house where you will shine.

It's where all your gifts will be put to use the way God intended them to be. His great grandparents, Abraham and Sarah helped God and got Ishmael, but he was not the heir God promised. Although God blessed him, Isaac was the promise and the two had to part ways. Even in their mess up, because of God's goodness their separation created a divine moment for Joseph to be ushered into the territory of his destiny. In God's hands, even our failures and mistakes work for our good when we love Him and are called by Him according to His purpose (Romans 8v28).

What can we learn from the Ishmaelite's arrival and what they brought?

1. They came on camels: Camels are animals that symbolize abundance of provision of something, from blessings, to love, and gifts. In Isaiah 60v6, they bring wealth and in Gen. 24v63, they bring Rebecca to marry Isaac. Their Hebrew symbol is Gimel or the third letter of the alphabet. Listen, Psalms 119v17-24 says about Gimel: *"Deal bountifully with thy servant that I may live and keep thy word. Open thou mine eyes that I may behold wonderful things out of thy law, I am a stranger in the earth; hide not thy commandments from me. My soul breaks for the longing that it hath unto thy judgments at all times. Thou hast rebuked the proud that are cursed, which do err from thy commandments. Remove from me reproach and contempt, for I have kept thy testimonies. Princes also did sit and speak against me; but thy servant did meditate on thy statutes. Thy testimonies also are my delight and my counselors."* Remember the lessons we learned in the pit? Look at the camels bringing confirmation to those lessons with encouragement and supplies that we will make it. Bountifully, living, and keeping God's word, opening of eyes (vision), they hate me, but I need you to heal me (remove the reproach). Princes sit and speak against me (his brethren sat and talked of him as they ate bread), but thy servant meditated on thy statutes (Faith at work and believing God's voice). Thy testimonies are my delight and counselors (I remember what you did for Noah, Abraham, Isaac and Jacob and I know you will keep me too).

2. They came from Gilead carrying spices;
   a) Gilead: a place known for its healing balms and ointments.
   b) Myrrh: an expensive spice used for perfume for kings, incense, medicine, and embalming. They symbolized the death of Canaan to Joseph for this period of his life. He would not see Canaan till he

returned to bury his father (and later his bones would be buried there). Joseph had to die to self and say goodbye to Canaan, as well. Sometimes we have to say goodbye to certain places and people in order for us to move forward in our destiny, not from the angle of hating people, but to focus on what we need to focus on. For Joseph, that included even his father whom he loved and admired. A spice for kings (King Xerxes and Jesus) is present in the midst of Joseph's pain to remind him that he is royalty and not forgotten. What seems like death is really the beginning of a powerful new chapter in Joseph's life. What God placed in him was about to shine like never before. Jesus was given myrrh at his birth and Esther was purified with myrrh before she was queen. What a powerful message for Joseph! In the midst of all his pain, God was heralding his special election to be a conduit of greatness.

c) Balm: Especially from Gilead, was used for healing purposes to wounds and also known as the healing balm of Gilead. God was bringing healing words for physical, emotional, and psychological wounds all inflicted by the people closest to him. Hurt from distant people or ones we don't know, may hurt, but not as deep as pain from those closest to us, especially family. Jesus is known as The Balm of Gilead who heals those deep wounds that have been inflicted by our loved ones, physically, emotionally psychologically, etc.

David cried out to God after experiencing the worst pain in these words in Ps. 55v12, "For it is not an enemy who taunts me, then I *could bear it; it is not an adversary who deals insolently with me, then I could hide from him. But it is you, a man, my equal, my companion, my familiar friend. We used to take sweet counsel together; within God's house we walked in the throng.*" (ESV).

When those who are closest to us hurt us, we experience the worst kind of pain. Pain is pain, but takes on a whole level of damage when it's close, because trust is violated and the place of safety in the nest is tainted. The psychological damage Joseph must have suffered, knowing the Philistines as bordering enemies would have been the ones to treat him this way or, surprisingly, would have treated him better than this. The Camels had to come to bring hope of healing on every level.

Reuben returns to find Joseph gone and is upset because he knows he's in trouble. I expand on the Reuben spirit later in chapter 15 and introduce him to you in whole different light in chapter four. Reuben represents power and leadership with a lack of responsibility. He has the right to rule, but shuns the depth of character that goes with it. He has a form of godliness, but lacks the power of it. In his failure to rule, we are introduced to a powerful new voice; one underdeveloped, but a leader at heart. He is not next in command by birth, but is a leader anyone can follow. He is anointed to speak well with reason and life even in the midst of his own mess and brothers' wickedness. Hello, Judah! There's something different about you, and we're going to see what it is.

Genesis 37v31-35: They took Joseph's coat, butchered a goat, and dipped the coat in the blood. They took the fancy coat back to their father and said, "We found this. Look it over—do you think this is your son's coat?" He recognized it at once. "My son's coat—a wild animal has eaten him. Joseph was torn limb from limb!" Jacob tore his clothes in grief, dressed in rough burlap, and mourned his son a long, long time. His sons and daughters (Genesis 37v35) tried to comfort him; but he refused their comfort. "I'll go to the grave mourning my son." Oh, how his father wept for him!

Proof of a dead promise

These men hated their brother so much that it was not enough that he was dead to them but had to be dead to everyone that knew him especially their father who loved him so much. It's not enough that your hater and accusers hate you in their own eyes; but with everything opportunity they get, they must slander your name and defame your character to everyone else. And like Joseph's brothers, they do it in such a sly, clever way that makes them look innocent. They present a blood stained, multi-colored coat to show your death and to show your failure. And you have now become the family's new example of failure.

They took his symbol of promise, anointing, and purpose, and dipped it in blood; goat's blood. What mockery! Interesting that it was goat's blood. In the end in the book of Revelation, it says that God will separate the sheep from the goats. They smeared his calling and reduced its value with mockery and logic of their own understanding, carnality, slander and hopelessness, void of God and rebellion, which is symbolized by the goat's blood. Others will hear your dreams and drench them in goat's blood. That's what has happened or will happen to you when you pursue your God-given dreams. (Side note: Levi particularly acted out of turn, even though it was way before his time. He didn't know what the spilling of a goat's blood would represent. When we don't know who we are, we abuse our resources. Our identity crisis will reflect in our stewardship. In the priestly order, goats were used for peace offerings, sin offerings, sweet-savor offerings and Passover (Exodus 12v5). For Asher, it represented health and it was permissible to eat and for good milk. Goat meat and milk are extremely healthy for you. With Zebulun, it was great for finance (Proverbs 27v26) and for Reuben it was a delicacy and needed it to be appreciated as one; Judges 6v19. (I will explain further in chapter 4).

Genesis 37v31-36: *[33]So they took Joseph's tunic, killed a kid of the goats, and dipped the tunic in the blood. Then, they sent the tunic of many colors, and they brought it to their father and said, "We have found this. Do you know whether it is your son's tunic or not?" And he recognized it and said, "It is my son's tunic. A wild beast has devoured him. Without doubt Joseph is torn to pieces." [34] Then Jacob tore his clothes, put sackcloth on his waist, and mourned for his son many days. [35] And all his sons and all his daughters arose to comfort him; but he refused to be comforted, and he said, "For I shall go down into the grave to my son in mourning." Thus his father wept for him. [36] Now the Midianites had sold him in Egypt to Potiphar, an officer of Pharaoh and captain of the guard."*

They present evidence of a blood-stained coat and notice it is Jacob who says with his own lips that his promised child is dead. This was the child and promise he had been longing for years. He holds, in his hands, the evidence of a dead dream in the blood- stained garment of his favorite son. Jacob had been made to believe that his dream was dead. Please note that you will come across people that will kill your dream and present your evidence that your dream is dead or will die eventually. They will present examples of statistics how there is no money in what you have been gifted to do. Countless examples of how cousin so and so tried that industry and fell flat on their faces or how it's a hobby but hobbies don't make money. Sound familiar? Listen, those moments of failure happened for them, but if God has called you to do something, it will succeed. Not saying that you won't face challenges or hurdles (they are designed to build Godly-character) but you must fulfill what God has called you to do despite the crowd that is not in your favor. Know that Heaven is and angels are waiting to serve and aid you to fulfill what God has called you to do. Jacob had been made to believe it was over and he refused to be comforted. Some encouraging thoughts:

1. When it looks like it's over: the blood was evidence. Has your dream been stabbed, wounded and left for dead? Not only was the dream and promise killed, so was Jacob's countenance and happiness. He tore his clothes, put on sackcloth and mourned. Some of you are mourning over lost dreams right now. Can I encourage you that the story is not over? Please keep reading. For Jacob, the promise he waited for over 20 years had slipped through his fingers because of a simple errand he wished he never sent Joseph on. Listen, it may look over, sound over and feel over with physical proof to validate it, but as the old folks say "it's not over, Baby, until God says it over."

2. They tried to comfort their depressed father. Please note that crushing a person's realm is no light matter. This is nothing that is easily fixed. Let us be careful what and how we speak to people concerning what God has placed inside of them. It is a precious miracle that God is sharing through that individual to the world. *"Your dream is God's love message to the world through you"* (Pastor Calvin J. Tibbs). It's an important assignment and so to crush it in someone is not a small matter. Trying to turn around and comfort them because you feel bad at the hurt you have caused or didn't realize you'd cause will not be an overnight endeavor. Let us be careful how we speak to one another.

3. Remember that Jacob was facing a wicked reality because there is power in dreams. Didn't he observe his son's second dream, even though he rebuked him for it? Yes he did. He was now mourning from a place of confusion and frustration. He was facing the worst pain a parent can feel, that of losing a child, and having to a dwell in that place of "But God you said". Had his son recited his dreams in error? Was he off about feeling that Joseph was special? Like you are living a life that is contrary to your dreams and promises and thinking, "what in the world happened? Did I miss something Lord? Your bills are increasing; your health is plummeting; the family is falling apart or disowning you; you name it. Do I have exciting news for you! You're on the path of an incredible turnaround. I know you don't see it, feel it, or maybe even sense it; but you have been placed on the road of abundant blessing. You are on the

47

highway of intense training and testing, that's all.

4. The Ishmaelites and Midianites were the hands and feet that carried joseph to his destiny. That's why it's important to bless your enemies and pray for them. God is using them to transition you into the next realm of glory. Someone had to do the dirty work to help you get to the next level. Somebody has to be the bad guy. Later, I will explain that elevation is not achieved in tranquility and the most comfortable of places, but your enemies, haters or strangers usher you there. Don't fight the process. It is birthed through affliction, adversity, pressure, heat and darkness. Don't despise your Judas (forgive him as Jesus did) because somebody needed to play the betrayer.

Joseph was taken to his place of destiny in the lap of luxurious comfort and taken straight to Pharaoh's palace for an internship. He was stripped of his beautiful coat, sold, re-sold and bought by Potiphar, Pharaoh's captain of the guard and head over his household affairs. We see the hand of God all over this situation; watching, orchestrating, guiding, planning and working. It has to be Potiphar:

1. An officer of Pharaoh – one of his officials –who served in the presence of Pharaoh and had access to Pharaoh. Sometimes devoted officials were called eunuchs even if they weren't. It was a title for those close and loyal to Pharaoh.

2. Captain of the guard: Head of the secret service, body guard and overseer of the affairs of Pharaoh's house. They went everywhere the king went and saw and heard everything. He made sure all was moving well in his house. He knew what he liked or didn't like. He was there to make Pharaoh's life as comfortable as possible. Joseph was strategically in a place where he would learn how to be an excellent leader under Pharaoh. He would learn the ways of Pharaoh and what pleased him and angered him. He got a front row view through the eyes of a slave, commoner and the elite. What a privilege!

3. Mrs. Potiphar was there. She plays an extremely important role in his elevation. Joseph received excellent training for what was coming ahead. A perfect way to learn to set boundaries when much is given to you! Greatness and compromise must always be ferocious enemies.

Chapter 4
Israel And Jacob:
God is working behind the scenes

This chapter has to be the most exciting one for me, because of the personal transformation the revelation has brought to my life. It is the very heartbeat of this book and brought me so much peace to the questions I had with the journey towards my destiny. It helped me change my entire attitude towards the trials of life and allowing patience to have her perfect way in my life. It clicked and a 180 degree turn happened in my life. I found myself saying a wholehearted yes to the Lord. HAVE YOUR WAY IN ME. I couldn't wait to write this chapter. And I pray it blesses you more.

From the time Joseph's brothers sold their brother, to the next time they saw him, he'd become the most powerful man in world. He who controls the money/food controls the world. Gen. 41v57; *"And all the other countries came into Egypt to Joseph for to buy corn; because that the famine was so sore in all lands."*

About 22 years passed, since he had his dreams of being a ruler. During that time a lot had happened. Of those 22 years, he spent 13 in intense training, about two back in Canaan and the rest in Egypt. In the following chapters, we will take a closer look at those 13 years and what we can learn from him and his brothers and how much we are like them. For those unfamiliar with the story, Joseph is now sold into slavery and serving the house of Potiphar, who is in charge of the Pharaoh's household and captain of the guard.

He then notices Joseph's remarkable work productivity, because the hand of the Lord is on his life and everything he touched prospered. He places Joseph over his household to manage all the affairs. After a while Potiphar's wife notices beautiful Joseph and plots to seduce him, but her plans don't work. Joseph resists her charms and in her rage, she wrongfully accuses him of alleged rape, causing him to be thrown into prison. This wasn't just any prison, but Pharaoh's prison where only he had the word of pardon for a prisoner be removed from there. In the dungeon, Joseph obtained favor with the prison guard who also elevated him to second-in-command in the prison. Here the Lord teaches him how to, not only dream, but interpret them and the dreams of others with great clarity. We see this when two of Pharaoh's servants are thrown into the dungeon and they have dreams that disturb them. Joseph, under the anointing of the Holy Spirit, interprets the dreams. One will be set free after three days and Joseph pleads for him to remember him and show him kindness.

The other was to be put to death after three days. Just as Joseph prophesied, so it was. The servant that was spared and reinstated to work for Pharaoh finally remembers Joseph two years later. Pharaoh has a couple of disturbing dreams and his wise men and counselors are not able to interpret the dreams. The butler remembers Joseph and word is sent from Pharaoh to bring Joseph out of the dungeon. Joseph, under the power of God in him, interprets the dreams with clarity and implements strategy as a problem solver. He is promoted to governor in Egypt, second in command. Nine years into his new position, Joseph is reconciled with his brothers and shortly after, his father and the rest of his father's household. So two things caught my attention that led to the revelation of this chapter:

1. Joseph had wealth and success and had the ability to head back to Canaan to see his father but he didn't. Why?
2. Jacob is not addressed as Israel until it is made mention or hinted that Joseph is alive (Gen 45v28). Why?

The answer to these two questions is the same. Jacob was called Israel but Israel had yet to be formed. Israel had 12 sons, who were 12 leaders, 12 destinies, 12 tribes, but one nation. As long as Joseph was around, he was the only son being mentored. When he was ready, God allowed the camels to take him ahead of the others to prepare a place for them to be nourished and sustained. Joseph, the dreamer and visionary in us represents the future that God has promised (Jer29v11). Joseph, now promoted to governor, had to be kept away because his coming back would have resulted in the underdevelopment of his brothers and thus the formation of Israel. As you pursue your dreams note this very important portion of scripture, *"Let patience have her perfect work in you." (James 1:4)*. Patience is heaven's highly recommended instructor and tutor for character development. It teaches us how to handle our dreams and be sustained in the land of plenty. It's not just about getting to the top; it's mainly about being able to live there. My father taught us that *"ability takes you to the top, but character keeps you there."* Each brother now needed to have time to spend with Jacob where he could mentor and train them to be all God had called them to be and what their destinies were ordained to be (Genesis 49).

Look in the mirror. I want you to see Jacob looking right back you. Yes, you are Jacob, standing tall and strong and chosen by God. God has also changed your name. He has called you [Spiritual] Israel, too. There are twelve parts to you that He has formed. There are twelve areas of leadership that you must put in their rightful place and twelve areas that you cannot ignore. You have favored your Joseph long enough: you have only been praying about your dream and neglecting the other components that you may not esteem too high, but are in you and of you. Let's take a look at the brothers and discover more about ourselves and why God is so concerned about each area.

◇◇◇

Gen. 49v3-4: *"Reuben, you are my firstborn, my might and the beginning of my strength, the excellency of dignity and the excellency of power. ⁴ Unstable as water, you shall not excel, because you went up to your father's bed; then you defiled it - He went up to my couch."*

REUBEN (Strong's H7205– Behold a son)

Reuben represents your soul. The soul houses your intellect, emotions and feelings and is a very important part of who you are. Common sense, the ability to sympathize, get angry, cry, mourn, drive a car, make friends, make judgment calls on what to wear, where to work, what to say, etc., all come from the soul.

It is a God-given part of you that has extreme power and daily guides your life into certain directions. Jacob describes him as the *beginning of his strength and his might*. He has the ability to get the job done, the anointing to be a leader and move the others forwards or backwards. But the Reuben in you is unstable. It can easily change its way of doing things in an instant because Reuben is power that settles to be good when it can be great. It defies boundaries because it is not principled. To some point, it can be very selfish and self- seeking. There are hints of good, but he can easily be persuaded to do evil. Because of his instability, he crosses boundaries and sleeps with his father's concubine. In so doing, he disrespects his father. But God has not given up on this first fruit. He sent Jesus to restore and reconcile him [the soul] to himself. I go into greater detail on the Reuben in us in chapter 15 and how sadly he is in more control than he should be.

◇◇◇

Gen. 47v5-7: *"Simeon and Levi are brothers; Instruments of cruelty are in their dwelling place. ⁶ Let not my soul enter their council; Let not my honor be united to their assembly; for in their anger, they slew a man, and in their self-will, they hamstrung an ox. ⁷ Cursed be their anger, for it is fierce; and their wrath, for it is cruel! I will divide them in Jacob and scatter them in Israel.*

SIMEON (Strong's H8095 – Heard)

Simeon represents the flesh in us. Not flesh, as in the tissue of your physical body, but rather the rotten, sinful nature in us that enjoys sin. Whenever given the chance, it thrives to do evil with its guiltless mind driving it forward with the desperate desire to be heard. It leads you down paths of unrighteousness and becomes silent when the consequences appear. While you're left thinking, "Oh no what did I just do?" the flesh has no desire to fix the problems it just created. There is nothing good about the flesh (Romans 7v18: *For I know that in me, that is in my flesh, dwells no good thing; for to will is present with me; but how to perform that which is good I find not.*). Simeon was one of the brothers that murdered Shechem and his men; even after his father Jacob had made peace with them and planned a way forward. Shechem had raped their sister. He was deeply in love with her and made truce with Jacob to set matters right and marry her. Jacob agreed but Simeon and Levi wanted blood.

Our flesh loves revenge. It is also self-seeking with no ounce of goodness or remorse. It is hateful, prejudice, murderous, rebellious, lustful, malicious, unkind, disloyal, loves adultery and fornication. When it is allowed to speak, it will, for it must be heard. It loves the platform and grows with every opportunity it is given to speak or shine. This is why Paul encourages us to mutilate and crucify it daily.

It's very much absorbed with ME and only wants what makes IT FEEL GOOD. Everything rotten about us, even our deepest darkest thoughts, resides in the flesh waiting for the opportunity to manifest. So, it's very interesting that when the brothers go to visit Joseph in Egypt and are not aware of his real identity, Joseph later imprisons them.

He releases them and keeps one as a prisoner. Can you guess who? Simeon; and that's where Simeon must be kept. When the promise or dream (Joseph) is reigning, the flesh (Simeon) must realize who's in charge; and place its self-proclaimed power in proper perspective. Put the Simeon in you in check before he expresses the potential of the evil in him. In those twenty years, Jacob was teaching Simeon how to be a part of Israel. Know your place, Simeon. Even though you are next in command after Reuben, you will never be in command. Later, when land in Canaan is given to the descendants of these 12 brothers, the tribe of Simeon is not given a place of their own. They were to dwell among and always within the borders of the tribe of Judah. (Joshua 19v1-9) Simeon, or the flesh in us must never be given the responsibility and privilege to make decisions; it must be crucified (Rom. 8v13, Gal. 5, 24, 1 Cor. 9v26-27) and silenced by the Judah in us. The flesh is not trustworthy and will land you in trouble all the time. It is evil and full of sin. Shut its mouth with the resurrected power of God and put it in the dungeon. Remember, this is the dungeon that the dreamer can thrive in, but not the flesh. Making decisions with this is extremely dangerous what we call fleshly.

◇◇◇

1 Chronicles 6v48-49:[48] *and their brethren, the Levites, were appointed to every kind of service of the tabernacle of the house of God.* [49] *But Aaron and his sons offered sacrifices on the altar of burnt offering and on the altar of incense, for all the work of the Most Holy Place, and to make atonement for Israel, according to all that Moses the servant of God had commanded.*

Roman 12v1: *I beseech you therefore brethren, by the mercies of God, that ye present your bodies a living sacrifice, holy, acceptable unto God, which is your reasonable service.*

◇◇◇

LEVI (Strong's H3878 – Joined to)

Out of the descendants of Levi, after the order of Moses and Aaron, was birthed the priesthood and the high priests. They were not allowed to participate in war nor have their own piece of land. Their only job as a tribe was to tend to the temple or tabernacle day and night. Therefore, Levi in us represents your actual physical body, primarily your hands and feet. Romans 12v1, says we are to offer up our bodies as a living sacrifice, meaning solely to join to the spirit within us and do the work of the Lord. We are not to join to Simeon or flesh nor live under the influence of Reuben. The body (Levi) is designed to join to a leader that needs a physical form in order to express itself. That's why Simeon took Levi with him to attack Shechem. Jacob cursed their unity and anger because it was a dangerous union. Our bodies must be vessels used for the glory of God ONLY.

◇◇◇

JUDAH (Strong's H3036 – Praised)

Judah was the fourth son of Jacob's not so favorite wife, Leah. At this point, she had stopped yearning for the love and sole attention of Jacob and purposed to praise God for blessing her with a fourth son. She called him Judah. Judah represents in us, our spirit man who is made with the sole purpose to praise and worship God. To live and reign with Jesus Christ! When we become saved, it is the part of us that lives in heavenly places and tabernacles with God in eternity. He speaks to it first even before our mind or soul is aware of what is going on (Ephesians). When we find Judah at the beginning of this story, he is very immature yet showing very strong signs of a leader (Genesis 37v26-27). When patience has her perfect way in our lives, Judah matures because Judah will be given Reuben's title of the first born (1Chronicles 5). As we progress in the story, we now see a mature Judah who is offering himself to be punished by his father if Benjamin is not returned safely to him when they visit Egypt.

As your dream is being perfected, so is your praise. You learn how to praise when God takes your Joseph to protect it. Joseph is enslaved and Judah is maturing; the promise is imprisoned and praise is growing. The promise is hidden whilst praise is being perfected. It must happen this way in us so that true worship is developed in us. Can we praise God in the valley when evidence of Joseph's death is before our eyes? Are we like Job and compelled to worship even in the worst of circumstances? Many praise God on the mountain tops and wonderful times. True worship, I believe, occurs when, like Shadrach, Meshach and Abednego, we choose to worship when there is the possibility that God may not rescue us from certain battles that lead to death. Praise is important because it has an inbuilt power and success. It unlocks doors that can't be opened by other means. When The Lord was creating the earth he had to say "it is good" or else for example the sun would get brighter and brighter. When He said the light was good He told the sun to not shine brighter than it did. Likewise as mini I am's in the earth when we worship we "say it is good" or "it is well" we speak with authority to say "that is enough". Praise also exalts the God of our lives to the throne of our hearts, the seat he deserves and in turn placing us at a place of humility. Humility is generously rewarded by God. While your dream is being perfected in the classroom of a dungeon, Judah is being transformed. Judah disliked Joseph with a passion, but loved him enough to spare his life. Little did he know how important Joseph was to his survival; that Joseph was chosen to sustain and nourish him, so that the Messiah, Jesus Christ, would come from Judah's line.

Judah is an immature worshipper at this point and this is dangerous. Immature worshippers speak death to their salvation, to their Kairos and to their household. When praise is self-seeking instead of God-focused, it behaves unwisely, entangled with unnecessary things, deceitful, lustful and judgmental. An immature worshipper is dangerous. Even its seed is immature and despicable, so much that God refuses it. The offering of Cain was such, sub- par and not of great quality (not the quantity but the quality).

When praise matures it produces exceptional the seed.

Immature praise:
- will be exposed so it can grow
- has no boundaries
- is highly judgmental
- makes stupid dangerous contracts not expecting any consequences
- easily parts with valuables based on lust
- does not keep it's word
- doesn't operate in love

Mature Praise:

- Has learned the sovereignty of God and humbles himself; Jesus was the King of Kings and the King of humility
- Esteems others higher than himself; Reuben offers his sons (Gen. 42v37) and Judah offers himself (Gen. 43v9)
- When backed up into a dangerous corner, he doesn't attack, but speaks in truth, authority, love and confidence (Gen. 44v18-34)
- Has a character that points to Christ (Gen. 4v10)
- Has the nature of a lion of a king; He is a force to be reckoned with; a lion, king of the jungle, majestic and triumphant with power for there is power in praise.
- He presents Jesus: restorer, forgiver, strength, kindness and humility
- Raises you up to always be the head and not the tail; always the leader God created you to be. (1 Chron.5v2)
- He lives a joyful life, no matter the circumstances because praise to God makes the heart glad. (Gen. 49v11,12 and Ps. 104v15)

Genesis 49v13: *Zebulun shall dwell at the haven of the sea; and he* shall be *for an haven of ships; and his border* shall be *unto Zidon.*

ZEBULUN (Strong's H2074 – Exalted)

Zebulun was blessed to go out and receive resources and bring them in; he had to be sharpened and matured to display an excellent work ethic and financial wisdom and responsibility. *[One of his borders is modern day Lebanon, previously known as Sidon.]*

- Had extensive commerce. A great city indeed
- Received name from Canaan's first son (Noah's great grandson)
- Commerce, manufacturers and the arts

In war, they supplied their brethren with weaponry, food and other supplies. They were very skillful, but mainly excellent with finances and business or trade. This represents, in you, the ability to manage your finances extremely well. God cares about how we handle our finances, our financial peace and ability to be a blessing to others in turn. It took wealth to build the temple and Jerusalem from the very start all the way through their rebuilding projects througho We are not less humble if we handle money well and prosper financ trouble comes when we love money and make it an idol. Part of your jou you learning how to handle your finances well and teach others to do so Especially the next generation entrusted to you [regardless of the nature in whic you influence their lives - parents, guardians, mentors, etc.]. Don't bury this gift God has given you. Question: How are you able to invest and multiply what's in your hand? Sharpening your Zebulun begins with embracing the knowledge that God promised to give us the power to obtain wealth (Duet 8v18). How you handle your finances is something that God cares about and wants to perfect in you as well. Let patience have her perfect work and way in your finances.

◇◇◇

Genesis 49v14-15: *Issachar is a strong donkey couching down between two burdens: And he saw that rest was good, and the land that it was pleasant; and bowed his shoulder to bear, and became a servant unto tribute.*

ISSACHAR (Strong's H3485 – There is recompense/reward)

When the mind is changed, the whole body follows. The tribe of Issachar is known for its sensitivity for and skill in discerning the times and seasons (1Chron. 12v32). Timing is everything. Issachar is your Instinct!!! This is the part of you that deals with your acute awareness of the times and seasons and how to act and not act, when to strike and when to lay low. The sons of Issachar were wise in the art of war, the law, and many areas of leadership being gifted with the awareness of the times designated to the season of a matter. Solomon writes on times and seasons in Ecclesiastes 3, so that instinct will know when to do what. Like how Mary knew exactly when Jesus was ready for first miracles and told the servants to do what Jesus told them to do. Please note, the major component of the Issachar anointing, is to have a servant's heart and ears. His father describes him as a strong donkey; an animal that is a beast of burden and used symbolically by Jesus as a sign for season shifts. (a. The donkey carrying Mary before Jesus is born; b. Jesus rides a donkey on Palm Sunday showing it's time for the ultimate sacrifice). The maturity of the Issachar in you will bring peace and contentment (not

___) as you go through different seasons of life; and therefore a natural ___ to keep in step with God, instead of going ahead of him. I can't wait to ___ y book on *The Issachar Anointing* that holds greater clarity on this part of ___ Look out for it!!!!

___ere are many who know their dreams, but missed their opportunity because their Issachar underdeveloped. The story of the ten virgins is a perfect example about instinct. The season and time for the bridegroom had arrived and instinct/Issachar had them prepare more than enough oil if the groom tarried. The five wise ones operated in Instinct (and were rewarded) and the five foolish missed their opportunity. Pay close attention sometimes to the hunches and gut feelings you get about certain evidence you cannot always explain. Another excellent read on this is Bishop T.D. Jakes' book, "Instinct." I highly recommend that as an intellectual and insightful source on the subject matter in order to be further educated on this part of you.

◇◇◇

Gen. 49v16-18: Dan shall judge his people, as one of the tribes of Israel. Dan shall be a serpent by the way, an adder in the path that biteth the horse heels, so that his rider shall fall backward. I have waited for thy salvation, O LORD.

DAN (Strong's H1835 – A Judge)

This is the part of us that makes judgment calls, governs and pleads causes. It works closely with instinct and your mind to move in a certain direction. It is the part of you that works with your logic or your spirit to strike whilst the iron is hot. This is your wisdom center that God wants to sharpen for his glory. This is the part of us the seats our mental and spiritual understanding and must be trained to exercise each well, knowing how to flow in and out of each. It is with skill and excellence that that this area knows how to use the knowledge it receives. Proverbs 4v7 says *"Wisdom is the principal thing; therefore get wisdom: and with all thy getting get understanding."* In order to execute judgment well, understanding of the circumstance is a prerequisite for the matter to be handled justly. How many times have we discredited people because we lacked understanding and wisdom on a matter or situation? Patience teaches us how to mature in this area.

◇◇◇

Genesis 49v19: *Gad, a troop shall overcome him: but he shall overcome at the last.*

GAD (Strong's H1410 - Troop)

Gad represents the warrior in you that refuses to give up. *"A troop overcame him but he eventually overcame it."* This is your will to fight. When this part dies or becomes discouraged, a person accepts everything and anything and lives a very defeated life. It is the power to keep fighting seen in the cloud of witnesses (Hebrews 12), the people of God that had every right to give up, but didn't.

- Paul and Silas in the prison
- Stephen being stoned
- Elijah running from Ahab and Jezebel
- Blinded Samson's God-given strength to kill the Philistines

This is the ability to fight back, when you feel there is no strength left in you. When we are weak, then we are strong. When we are poor, we are rich. It's the grace of God that allows us to be more than conquerors. Our strength is God's joy in us, the power of his might. It is our will power, our beliefs, and our inner fight to live; the place that houses adrenaline (fight or flight). Deuteronomy 6v5 states that we are to love God with all our strength. God puts his super on our natural to walk on the storms, to lay aside the weight and sin that easily set us back. This is another important area that God cares so much about and wants to develop in you. The place that pushes past the press! The press is the place of extreme pressure, where it is easier to make peace that a situation may not change (The Shunammite woman accepted not having a son) but the word of God comes with encouragement to push past that place of extreme pressure with the strength of His grace.

◇◇◇

Genesis 49v20: *Out of Asher his bread shall be fat, and he shall yield royal dainties (Strong's H4574 - food).*

ASHER (Strong's H836 – Happy)

Asher deals with our health. God cares about that too. He wants us to eat well and be physically nourished well, so much that he made a promise to us in Matthew 6 that he will take care of that for us. The foods we put into our bodies must be given thought, because the sole purpose is to give us fuel to function. God has blessed us with the opportunity to enjoy the fuel we eat but sin has caused us to misuse that blessing so that we mistreat God's image of food and the relationship it has with our bodies. We have emotional eating, over eating, under eating, fattening foods, diets, etc. Jesus taught us to pray to ask our Father to give us daily bread (His grace in action even after the fall). Health covers a number of things such as sickness, disease, weight loss, being whole, etc. Although our identity is not based on how we look, we must be able to take great care of our bodies and health to the best of our ability. It's a journey and for some it takes longer than others, but no matter where you are, know that you are not alone and God cares about your health. Allow patience to mature you to take care of your temple. *(3 John 2: Beloved, I wish above all things that thou mayest prosper **and be in health**, even as thy soul prospereth.)* Jesus died on the cross for our health, healing and wholeness.

Genesis 49v21: *Naphtali is a hind let loose: he giveth goodly words.*

NAPHTALI (Strong's H5321 – Wrestling)

Naphtali represents our tongue or speech, one of the smallest members of our bodies, but has a lot of power in it. For being so small it wrestles many things and has the power to steer our entire lives in the path it chooses. Constructive and destructive power is packed in those tiny cells. The Bible also describes it as having the power of life and death. Having a tongue that is matured in Christ is extremely important. An unbridled tongue can prevent one from going into their destiny or whereas a matured one ushers them right into it. Take for example Moses (Num.20v12); by using his tongue in rage he expressed the frustration in his heart and he was not allowed to enter the Promised Land with Joshua, Caleb and the Children of Israel.

He later set foot on it on Mount Nebo (Deut.34) because God had made a promise to him that he would see the land. Our tongue, as the smallest member of our body, has the power to direct the whole body according to James, just as a steer guides the whole ship (James 3v3-5). As patience has her perfect work in us, it matures the tongue too, making it mature to guide the whole body. Do you want to receive your break through or answer to prayer or promise only to lose it because of an immature tongue? God loves you too much to let you do that to yourself [again], to let you lose your Eden because of an untrained tongue. In the well- known verse of Jeremiah 29v11, God says that He has good thoughts or plans towards us, thoughts to prosper us and bring us hope and an expected end. Don't despise this time where it feels like you have been forgotten. You are in preparation. Your speech is being seasoned with salt (Col.4v6). God is removing the negative, lifeless, backbiting, conceited, malicious, lying, murdering speech out of your tongue. The Spirit is teaching you how to control your tongue and engage it into life-giving, prosperous, positive, Biblical inspired speech. For some the struggle is being opinionated, or not speaking up enough, telling half-truths, gossip, etc. Let the Spirit of God transform your tongue.

Our speech must be life giving at all times. Our speech gives life to our dreams so we have to learn how to speak life. Also, if our speech is not corrected we do more damage to others we have to lead when we are in positions of power. Bad leaders, bad parents and bad bosses use their untrained tongues to speak death to those entrusted to their care. It also involves what you allow yourself to hear and be told. Don't allow negativity to come into your eye and ear gates. Glean from Asher too, for spiritual health what you are eating spiritually. That helps Naphtali work well because if it is in your heart it will come out through your speech and actions. It involves what you allow yourself to hear and ingest. What voices are you listening to? Good words, words of life and creative power are to flow into you so they can flow out of you. Be careful of your company. Get up from the seat of the scorners and out of the path of the wicked. Don't walk in the counsel of the ungodly (Psalm 1).

◇◇◇

Genesis 49v22-26: *Joseph is a fruitful bough, even a fruitful bough by a well; whose branches run over the wall: The archers have sorely grieved him, and shot at him, and hated him: But his bow abode in strength, and the arms of his hands were made strong by the hands of the mighty God of Jacob; (from thence is the shepherd, the stone of Israel:) Even by the God of thy father, who shall help thee; and by the Almighty, who shall bless thee with blessings of heaven above, blessings of the deep that lieth under,* *blessings of the breasts, and of the womb: The blessings of thy father have prevailed above the blessings of my progenitors unto the utmost bound of the everlasting hills: they shall be on the head of Joseph, and on the crown of the head of him that was separate from his brethren.*

◇◇◇

JOSEPH (Strong's H3130 – Jehovah has added)

The dreamer in you is your Joseph. It is your life's core purpose and mission and explained throughout this book. This is the part that we, like Jacob, mostly focus on or totally ignore. It is birthed through adversity, rejection, and trials. It requires determination, stamina, and pressing through the odds stacked against it. Jehovah has added this part to you to sustain and nourish every part of you on your journey here on earth. He adds this so that fruit (Judah) can be sustained on the branch (Joseph) that is provided. That's why your dream cannot die this season and you MUST fight for it to be birthed into the earth. Age is not a disqualifier for this, neither is gender, class, or whatever you have concluded disqualifies you to fulfill your God-given dreams. Who God says you are is what counts. His report is the final say so. DREAM!!!!!!

◇◇◇

Genesis 49v27: *Benjamin shall raven as a wolf: in the morning he shall devour the prey, and at night he shall divide the spoil.*

BENJAMIN (Strong's H1144 – Son of the right hand)

This represents our will power and victorious nature and leader in you. What our will sets out to do, it will be accomplished. A wolf sees its prey and knows what it wants and pursues it till it's caught. God gave us will power not only for the freedom of choice but to also exercise the ability/power to go after what we want. What do you want? What are you passionately pursuing? You have been equipped with will power to pursue and successfully achieve victory. It is faith active in your life as the substance of things hoped and evidence of things not seen (Hebrews 11:1). Faith is what pleases God and moves his hand to do the impossible. We have been given the power to have dominion in the earth. We have been given the power to choose victory. Even those that don't walk with God put their will to a certain task it comes through. It is a God-given gift given without repentance because it is an example of his image and likeness that we are made in. The right hand is known for power, and strength and might. It signifies success and victory. Patience matures God's strength in our lives. Also, your Benjamin is the power of your name. His mother in bitter sorrow during childbirth named him Ben-oni (Son of my sorrow) but Jacob changed it to Benjamin (son of my right hand). What does your name mean? It is linked to your destiny. What it means will explain a lot about who you are and what you do. Don't be discouraged if your name doesn't have the greatest meaning; take a page out of Jabez's book (whose name meant sorrow or bitterness). He asked the Lord to change his life for the better despite the meaning of his name.

At the Jordan

Jacob forming into Israel is not an overnight transition, but let me encourage you with this: the power of the twelve is extremely important and together they accomplish much and stand strong. Their victories are clearly seen throughout scripture. One of my favorite books in the Bible is Joshua and it shows the power of the twelve in full effect. In chapter four, the Ark of the Covenant held by the priests has gone forth before them into the Jordan River and is held by the priests in the midst of the Jordan. Twelve leaders of each tribe were to find a boulder and place it in the middle of the Jordan for a memorial to teach their children that God had brought them this way and delivered them from years of slavery in Egypt. To say that *"Israel came over this Jordan on dry land...That all the people of the earth might know the hand of the Lord, that it is mighty..."*(Joshua 4v22-24). Joshua also built a memorial altar in the midst of the Jordan that the waters would cover once the priests and the Ark of the Covenant passed clear over onto the other side of the Jordan. A complete Israel would be used to build many altars together, win many battles, and claim a land for their inheritance as a whole.

Chapter 5
The Power of Biblical Reconciliation

I wonder if the brothers had approached their father about his favoritism, would this story have gone a different way. Isn't it interesting that the anger meant for their father was lashed out on poor Joseph. When favor is evident upon a life, expect people's frustration to not be directed to God, but expressed through jealousy to the recipient of the favor. Joseph never asked to receive this favoritism and like all of us, never had a say so in whom he was born of. He found himself in a position to receive favor.

Although the Lord used everything ugly about this situation for the good of his people, there is something to be learned even from the character and hatred displayed by Joseph's brothers (who also represent certain ones in the body of Christ). We can't help but realize that there are many Christians being severely mistreated by other believers. Saints leave churches, not because of God, but the people who are God's or claim to be His. But why, what causes these attitudes from people? What makes people smile in your face one day and hate your guts the next? What causes someone to hate on you instead of rejoicing or sympathizing with you, especially Christians? Our inner man has not dealt with the following:

1. Jealousy and envy are real
2. Lack of knowledge and identity in Christ
3. Ignorance (lack of belief in one's dream and purpose)
4. Spiritual immaturity (no spiritual growth)
5. Carnality (a mind not subjected to The Lord)

Genesis 45:1-8

For Joseph to weep before them instead of hating them and really letting them have it, shows his heart of forgiveness and love for his brothers. That forgiveness towards them had happened a while ago. Probably in the dungeon of nothingness, God visited this young dreamer/seer about his destiny and the part his brothers had to play. Forgiveness is a powerful thing that allows you to live freely in the will of God. Unforgiveness will not grant you that. Joseph realized that God used the hands of his brothers to send him to Egypt where God would promote him to save many. The process to promotion was just as important, so how he went there mattered just as equally. Nothing escapes God at all and His sovereignty is so incredible, and way beyond our understanding, that it leaves us with no doubt but to trust Him. It was important that Joseph went to Egypt as a slave, the lowest position possible so that he could learn the culture quickly and well; and also for God to receive all the glory in his promotion. Our anointing and gifting packages make it easy for us to give receive the credit for promotion and advancement in our endeavors. So God allows the journey to promotion to be challenging to save us from ourselves.

If Joseph had gone there as a distinguished dignitary (nothing wrong with that) a part of us would be convinced his status made way for him. We understand that to start at the bottom and be raised up like Joseph was, solely required the hand and power of God. And so, God is glorified! It's actually more exciting and sends a mighty blow of shame to the enemy because he anticipated the pit to kill us. Because of his willingness, we watch and glean from his exciting journey.

Concerning reconciliation, I hear the Lord saying this to you, the reader; *"Tell them of Philemon v18 which says, 'If he hath wronged thee, or owes thee ought put that on my account." For the believers, especially they that have wronged you, I will repay it." Forgive them. Release them by, knowing what they did to you, I allowed it to further develop what is in you. I will use that situation for your good and for my glory. You will see progress as we walk together. I am sovereign enough to do that. Nothing catches me by surprise, I know all things way before they happen and I have it all under control. I have sent my Spirit to help you forgive. I'm not telling you to get over it as if something serious didn't happen to you, but rather please allow me to do something wonderful in you by using even those painful things to polish the gold in you. I allowed it because I know of the good I would bring out of it. Don't hold bitterness. Know that like the pearl, I allow the rough grains of the sand to rub against it to polish and smooth the pearl. I was forming the pearls of your life so that you would be handled with care and not cast yourself, gifts or anointing before swine or people that will trample and destroy you or them. Because I am judge, I know the conditions of men's hearts. Pharaoh's heart was easily hardened towards Moses because of his type of heart. Joseph's brother's hearts were melted later because of their type of hearts. I know all and see all. Love those that hate you, bless those that curse you and remember that vengeance is mine. Know I've got you and will redeem your honor."*

It is important for us to know that people, saved or unsaved, hate what they are ignorant and afraid of. Joseph was a threat to his brothers because as long as he was around they feared a long term distance from Jacob. Jesus taught that a prophet is not welcome in their own home. Joseph lived a life of excellence. He was exceptional and the glory and hand of God rested very strongly on his life. It was evident by the dreams he had. The problem is that anytime we stand out, we become a target for the enemy and people, saved and unsaved. They want us to stay in their comfortable bubble which, in their eyes is greatness. They maliciously put you down in either blatant, cunning, or deceitful ways because your greatness makes them uncomfortable.

As I write this chapter, I think of how much I relate to this treatment and how it almost broke me and made me want to give up. BUT GOD! I am blessed to have the support of an incredibly loving and super supportive family, but too often found myself mistreated in the relationships outside of it. I have learned to say, *"Father, forgive them for they know not what they do.".* It brings me great joy knowing that all those hurts were for a powerful purpose. It was to make me more like Jesus and bring me to my expected destiny that God has prepared for me. They helped shape me in some way or another. I will not allow my fire to be quenched. My mind is made up to follow God despite the naysayer and in turn love them all the same. They are simply a tool God is using to perfect me. WOW! What a perspective. It makes it easier to love and pray for them. I am not afraid of the pit or the dungeon. They, too, are tools used to sharpen our character. Hallelujah! I decree the same for you; that you will be rise above the trespasses and bless when it's easier to curse.

The trouble I have today is how conflict is being handled. Even though the word is clear and plain on this, sadly there are many other versions of truth on this matter floating around. Somehow, gossip, in the fashion of prayer requests has risen. Silent hatred, silent treatment, slander form the pulpit, condescending rebuke, etc. are ways being pursued to resolve conflicts amongst us. I'd like to focus on Joseph's life, coupled with a scripture from the New Testament, showing that God has a way for conflict resolution to happen under grace. I believe there is a greater revelation on this matter as we only know in part, but these are the things I notice about Joseph:

Joseph becomes transparent:

A. Genesis 45v1: Joseph refuses to show animosity or keep a harsh front before his brothers. Instead, he loves them dearly despite all they did to him. He makes himself vulnerable to them by weeping before them when he has all the power to destroy them. He puts aside his title as governor and shows himself as a peer. Don't use power and prestige to prevent you from being open with the people you are to be transparent with.

B. He removes all parties that are not involved in the issue, squabble or disagreement. Meet alone with the offender before you go running to leadership or third parties. (Mat.18v15-20) Take a witness a second time if nothing was resolved. Then see the leadership if nothing is still resolved. If that individual or individuals do not show remorse after that, they must be asked to leave the church. At that point, it is clear that they have an unteachable and rebellious spirit. This is a spirit that is very dangerous to the body. It is like a cancer and can be taught and passed on to others.

C. It must be done in a loving manner lest you fall into the same situation. Never esteem yourself so high and mighty that you can't fall into the same sin you are rebuking others over. There has to be absolutely no condemnation when we are instructing others when rebuking them. Joseph gently restored his brothers by lovingly reassuring them as men of God. He didn't tear them down as wretched sinners who deserved death for selling him into slavery.

D. He used spiritual understanding to forgive his brothers. The bigger picture was that this was not about Joseph and the wrong that had been done to him, but rather Joseph being positioned to honor a covenant God made with Abraham and over all that God had spoken in the beginning. Spiritual understanding is a powerful tool freely given for us to use to see in the spiritual realm what God is doing. Have the eagle's eyesight (bigger, clearer picture) it brings clarity to the situation.

E. True forgiveness is not pretentious. His brothers were convinced that, after their father died, Joseph would show his true colors. Joseph had been trained by God to be faithful and be of noble character in the dungeon where it was easy to be bitter. Forgiveness has no hidden motives and agendas. It is pure freedom and continues in kindness well into eternity. It is not conditional, but is subjected to the Lordship of Jesus Christ.

Joseph identified and dealt with his hurt:

Joseph, felt the hurt his brothers had bestowed on him and we see by him weeping that he was dealing with the pain. It's not just about recognizing it and letting it sit there exposed and fresh. That's why we find it hard to forgive. We excel at making our mind aware of the offence only but Jesus came to teach us what to do with a known offence.

A. Joseph wept in private and in public (identified the pain)
B. Joseph released his hurt to God (released the pain)

Very good for cathartic release and brings inner healing.

Genesis 45v3: *"and Joseph said unto his brethren, I am Joseph; does my father yet live? And his brethren could not answer him, for they were troubled at his presence."*

Joseph was concerned about other parties hurt by the offense:

A. Joseph would have let them deal with the conviction of what they did to him and him alone, but he doesn't want them doing that. He knows he left a father who was living life with certain unanswered questions. Forgiveness takes the focus of ourselves and seeks to build others who are involved. His father, spiritual father, his mentor was in Canaan thinking Joseph was dead and here Joseph wanted to immediately put a smile back in his heart

B. His brothers' world had been turned upside down. Blood pressures were skyrocketing and condemnation was settling in. Guilt, shame and fear were running a relay race all in the short time of when Joseph revealed himself. In verse 4-6, Joseph draws them to himself to assure them of his love and forgiveness. It was God who brought Joseph to Egypt and not them. Joseph wanted them to see the bigger picture, too, and give glory to God. He first had to forgive them so he could teach them to forgive. You go through offense so you can learn freedom of forgiving and, in turn, teach others how to be free.

Joseph understood forgiveness and justification:

My parents taught me that we often confuse forgiveness with justification. Forgiving and forgetting is justification. It is what God does with us and, on occasion, gives us the grace to do with others. Forgiveness on the other hand is letting the offense go, knowing God has a bigger plan but not necessarily forgetting. For example a convicted criminal who has served their time for stealing has slim to no chances of handling money in a corporate or ministry setting but will help in other areas. Whereas justification says absolutely you get a second chance you are chief financial officer. It helps to know that some people have hurt and offended you not because of something you did but rather because of who they are. They weren't mean to YOU, they are mean. They weren't unkind to YOU, they are unkind. It helps not take it personally.

Joseph set the pace for God's will to be done (Gen. 45v 6-22)

What God had intended was now set into motion. What is your unforgiveness blocking? Are you fighting against God? After Joseph forgave his brothers, the house of Pharaoh heard they were in Egypt. Pharaoh was delighted to meet the family of his highly esteemed official and offered to give them the best of the best. It was a way of Pharaoh showing gratitude to Joseph. He couldn't wait to bless them and give them the best of the land. He couldn't wait to pour back into Joseph and return the appreciation he felt towards Joseph for being a blessing to Egypt and himself. Forgiveness opens doors!!!

Chapter 6
Favor and Prosperity - more than money

et's back track to Genesis 39 where the story continues and we see that the favorite son has been sold into slavery and is serving the house of Potiphar. Joseph is taken out of the picture (from Jacob's perspective) so that the dream can be worked on and perfected behind the scenes. You are not forgotten. God is fighting on your behalf and working it out for your good.

God alone evaluates your dream (Gen.39 v1)

Joseph finds himself sold not once, but twice. Low monetary values had been placed on his head by those closest to him and by strangers (Ishmaelites who were distant relatives). Talk about the enemy sending a message of worthlessness.

Knowing who you are in God is vital and is the foundation of a victorious life no matter where you are. It determines the outlook of your life, drives decision making and shapes your world. If we don't allow God to define us, anyone will. Everything around us is driven to feed the need of a consumer society. Wants are daily becoming needs due to cleverly calculated marketing or by the progressing development of life and technology. I remember when cell phones were once a luxury, but now are necessities to conduct business, ministry, communication etc. Millions of dollars are being pumped into research departments of companies to study the market demographics. They study consumption, trends and conversations on social media to see what the consumers' needs and wants are.

Like Joseph people will place a price over your head. They will do things to try to determine your value and worth or that of your dream or vision; but an amazing price has already been placed on your life. The only price that counts is the blood of Jesus Christ shed on Calvary. Don't cheapen yourself because of a low price that has been placed on your head by others or yourself for that matter. The shame of a failed marriage, a rebellious child, loss of a job, questionable past, or guilt of an abortion are prices of worth the enemy marks over your head. Make the great exchange today and embrace the price Jesus paid for you. Stand strong in Christ! Knowing who you are in Him is sealed and precious to him.

Someone took the time to create and fashion you. He made you out of His own image. You are an expression of the mind of God. Only the Master has the blue print of your life and he alone knows your true worth. Please don't designate that right to anyone else but God. People come and go, change, adapt or rebel. You cannot place so huge a responsibility on such inconsistency. Your free will (Benjamin) allows you the right to choose who will be Lord over your life. He will reveal his dreams for your life that are far greater than what we can think or imagine for ourselves. So protect your dream and cast down the words of naysayers mocking it. Have a mental baseball bat that knocks negative words and insults out the ball park. They don't have to know what happened, just internally refuse the "no" because God has already said "yes." Not every battle is won with words.

Joseph is reduced to 'nothing,' and brought DOWN to Egypt and purchased. He is re-introduced to the twin brothers "demotion and devalued" who have waxed in malevolence and strength; and brought along their baby sister "loneliness."

A different look at prosperity
I said all that earlier to say this, we see Joseph at a very low place in his life. He is low in every area, especially financially and materially. He only had the clothes on his back, literally, to call his own. Yet this season of his life, Joseph is described as prosperous or having the spirit of prosperity.

We've often heard it said that having prosperity is being wealthy or being money related. But prosperity in Biblical definition is not being wealthy and should the two not be used synonymously. Having wealth and money is not sinful but the love of the two is what is. Finances are important and are available through employment, inheritances, etc. to generate income which we use to provide necessities such as food, clothing, shelter, transportation, education, and so on. Wealth is a subject under the umbrella of prosperity.

Prosperity is the God-given privilege to succeed at everything entrusted in our hands. It must not be limited to increase in wealth. The New Testament mentions it as doing well and succeeding in *3 John 1:2, "Beloved, I wish above all things that you may prosper and be in health, even as your soul prospers.* I'm not belittling finances in this book. To do so would be to devalue the Zebulun in you. I believe finances are a blessing from the Lord that must be used to give a worthy account to the Lord. It is a blessing from the hand and presence of God that brings productivity, fruitfulness and dominion. In Gen. 1v28, the Lord blessed man with prosperity. He instructed him to be fruitful, to multiply, replenish the earth, subdue it and have dominion over it.

- Fruitful: producing fruit, offspring and vegetation especially in abundance. Producing useful or desired results.
- Multiply: to increase the amount, number, or degree of; to perform multiplication of.
- Replenish: to make full or complete again by supply for what is lacking or has been used up.
- Subdue: to conquer and subjugate, vanquish, to bring under cultivation, to quiet, bring under control by physical force or persuasion.
- Dominion: control or exercise control, sovereignty, rule, area of control, sphere of influence, authority.

(Freedictionary.com)

"The Lord was with Joseph and he was a prosperous man; and he was in the house of his master the Egyptian."

(NT) Luke 11v13 *"If ye, being evil, know how to give good gifts unto your children: how much more shall your Heavenly Father the Holy Spirit give to them that ask him?"*

Joseph is described as prosperous (what we understand as wealthy, well-to-do and comfortable) but this young man is a slave and managing the house of his Egyptian master. At the end of the day, these material blessings were not his, but only left his care, yet he is still described as prosperous. This makes me look at prosperity in a whole different light than limiting it to wealth. Joseph, who was stripped of everything, was described as prosperous because the evident presence of God was on his life. God being seen in and on our lives is prosperity; or the manifestation of His right hand. *(May His prosperity to be seen on your life)* It is that anointing to succeed at all that we do. Our dream is designed to succeed. When you find yourself living your dream, it will succeed because it comes pre-packaged with that anointing.

In Gen 49v22-26, we see that Joseph is blessed with prosperity by his father. Your God given dream, purpose, destiny and future are blessed with prosperity and that's why the enemy wants to steal, kill, and destroy it. It is birthed out and inspired by the image of God.

A. Fruitful: *Joseph is a fruitful bough, even... by a well: had the ability to duplicate, produce results, is effective, a leader, a productive, has favor, reliable*

B. Multiply: *whose branches run over the wall: [multi-gifted]*

C. Replenish: v25 *"Even by the God of their father, who shall help thee; and by the Almighty, who shall bless thee with blessings of Heaven above, blessings of the deep that lies under, blessings of the breasts, and of the womb."*

D. Subdue: v23-24 *"The archers have sorely grieved him, and shot at him, and hated him; but his bow abode in strength, and the arms of his hands were made strong by the hands of the mighty God of Jacob (from thence is the Shepard, the Stone of Israel."*

E. Dominion: v26 *"The blessings of thy father have prevailed above the blessings of my progenitors (a biologically related ancestor or founder of a family)unto the utmost bound of everlasting hills; they shall be the head of Jacob and on the crown of the head of him that was separate from his brethren."*

Image of God → Identity→ Prosperity → race well run/assignment completion

"Prosperity is the truth dimension, the place where we strive to live and the place that comes after a disciplined life." - Bishop Tudor Bismark

Whoa, I love that. What a powerful statement that is. Joseph under his Father's roof had started living a living of discipline already. What a testimony at such a young age. Young person don't let anyone tell you, you are too young to live a holy, disciplined and magnificent life in Christ; or too young be used by God. There are many examples of young people God used to do incredible things and make a difference in the earth.

So this place requires discipline, which is mainly taught in trials and tribulations. But is also exercised by an individual that decides to live in the spirit of excellence; which I want to expand on a little bit. The spirit of excellence is in Joseph but broken down step by step in the Daniel 1. The first thing Daniel did was purpose in his heart that he would not defile himself with the king's meat (offered to and marinated in the blood of Babylonian enemies) and wine. To eat at someone's table or share a meal with them meant you agreed with their lifestyle. Daniel made this statement to set himself apart from ungodly Babylonian customs. The Lord had told them in Jeremiah 29 to settle in Babylon for 70 years or so of their captivity. But Daniel purposed in his heart that his settling would still honor the Lord.

The spirit of excellence continues in him continued by him honoring leadership in requesting to eat differently. Remember having a conviction is not grounds for rudeness and insubordination. His conviction was honored because he promised results for what he believed. That's another element of the spirit of excellence. Let your life show fruit of what you are convicted by. Don't make noise, produce fruit! Your speaking up for your convictions will also encourage others in doing the same (Shadrach, Meshach, and Abednego). This is the sprit that rested in and on Joseph and Daniel.

It's a place of purpose, productivity, excellence and dominion. The Holy Spirit is the author of the spirit of excellence. Living in him you are positioned to live by the principles these two men lived by. He is success. He is successful living. That's why Jesus said that if men, being wicked, give good gifts, how much more would God the Father give the Holy Spirit? The Holy Spirit is the greatest gift anyone can be given. Embrace Him today and begin a life of prosperity. Everyone's 'Joseph' stage is different. For some it's 40 years, some it's weeks, maybe even a year, but we must be prepared to live there. When it seems that God has forgotten, He hasn't. He is perfecting all that concerns us or the Israel in us. He is aware of all and sends your dream ahead of you so that you are sustained (Ps. 105v17).

May the presence of God and the spirit of prosperity rest so heavy on us that it is evident to all and specific key people around us. This leads me to my third point.

Favor from God gives us grace/favor with man (Gen 39v4-5)

The goodness of God is amazing for so many reasons and this happens to be one of them. Out of His goodness, He chooses us. Favor with man can only be obtained when we have obtained favor with God. Favor with God does not happen or occur based on how good we are or faithful we are, rather because of how good God is. His love that He has lavished on us is indescribable. When He pours His goodness on us, it is something we can't explain. He poured His goodness, glory and presence on Joseph. Excellence, eloquence of speech, authority, dignity and purpose naturally flowed out of him. Everything he set to do prospered and produced great results. Not just for results, but great results. He produced something this world is slowly losing sight of, quality. The masses have growing needs, and our microwave society wants everything 'yesterday,' so quantity has overridden quality. With Joseph, he produced quality work and results and that got the attention of his master. He operated in the wisdom of God. Every time your hands and words are put to your creativity, power begins to flow. Every time creative power is flowing, wisdom and understanding are required.

- Proverbs 3v19: '*By wisdom the Lord laid the earth's foundations by understanding he established the heavens.*"
- Made in his image we must flow in wisdom and understanding to operate effectively in creative power, and it is ours for the asking
- Proverbs 2v6: "*The Lord gives wisdom, out of his mouth comes knowledge and understanding.*"
- James 1v5: "*If any of you lack wisdom, let him ask of God that giveth to all men liberally, and upbraided not, and shall be given him.*"

What does this favor from God and noticeable to man look like? When the Lord rests on our lives and we surrender to the Lord our lives display a radiant, attractive light of glory. It is visible to the natural eye, not always Shekinah glory, but the evidence of wisdom, in all things; excellent work ethic, productive projects, impeccable insight, outstanding character, all coupled with amazing humility. This is known as *CHAYIL* glory. The same glory that rests on the Proverbs 31 woman! Potiphar was able to see tangible evidence that Joseph's life was kissed by the favor of God. A couple of things must be pointed out though (and some as a reminder). What did Potiphar see? :

1. Joseph was a poor slave with rich character – he had every right to be bitter and angry with the life and God and yet showed an unwavering excellence and fruit of the Spirit (Gal. 5:22-23).

2. He was a hard and effective worker – depression could have set in and caused him to give up on life, but he operated in the joy of the Lord. It gave him strength and he was a man of action. He got the job done with efficiency.

3. He had an excellent spirit in stewardship: He treated another man's belongings with great care and respect. He did not bury it, mistreat it or be intimidated by it. He worked as if unto the Lord. His father had taught him this when he was a boy in the manager position in his house.

4. He had a pleasant attitude: whatever attitude we embrace is contagious. Smile from your heart. It's a shame to be so accomplished and be the worst person to be around. This was not the case with Joseph. He was pleasant and a joy to serve with. People like Stephen had Shekinah glory rest on their face in the midst of being stoned. When others would have cursed; he blessed. Choose to be joyful! It actually helps us more when we have a good attitude about what we face in life. It also keeps complaining away because we learn to be content, in little or much.

5. He had positive conversation: what a man thinks so is he in his heart (Prov. 23v7 and Luke 6v45) for out of the abundance of his heart, his mouth speaks. He built others up and motivated them to be better.

6. He was a leader: He was influential, great with people, inspiring, encouraging and a motivator. Potiphar put him in charge of all in his house (that includes the other slaves)
   - Esteem others above yourself (servant heart)
   - Speak the truth in love (firm, kind, edifying, not rude)
   - When you truly love God you must love people (Christianity is that, 1Jn. 4v7-11, 20,21)
   - Goes the extra mile
   - A man of power
   - A man of humility
   - Intelligent and trained well (by Jacob)
   - Substance and culture
   - A man of determination

7. He lived a life of purpose (prophetic, hope, future, vision); when you know your purpose in life, it gives direction for today to aid tomorrow. It annihilates what the struggles of today try to determine or define the final say about you. The struggles of today are only tools to sharpen you for your amazing future. Joseph's walk was different. He had pep in his step because slavery was not the final say. He had a dream he was holding onto. Even though no one else believed it, he did, because he believed in God and God was a covenant keeper. When you have purpose and destiny, you are not defined by today's circumstances. You have the walk of a conquering warrior, because you know you are working towards a goal. It's like you have insider information on life or the future so today's trials and setbacks don't throw you completely off. You may fall, but you get up and keep running. It becomes the life force to motivate and drive you to keep going. What is your purpose?

8. He is a man of discipline and boundaries: In order for someone to entrust you with something, they also need to see your discipline in the area of boundaries. It is the language of respect, knowing that crossing certain lines is gravely frowned upon. He understood what he was responsible for and excelled at it. This topic is another book on its own, but in short, when you respect someone or something, boundaries will not be easily crossed.

Joseph is unquestionably a remarkable young man anyone wouldn't mind having on their team. So let the Joseph anointing flow out of you. Apply the traits that caused him to find grace in the eyes of Potiphar and see the how much the quality of your life changes for the better. In Gen. 39v21-23, the favor Joseph experiences here is the favor where God speaks to a person or persons on your behalf. They have a strong liking for you without having much evidence of your history or current circumstances. They have a natural, quick liking to you based on the unction or nudging by the Holy Spirit. You can't explain it, so embrace it.

Don't exploit it. It is built on trust. For Joseph, the prison ward entrusted all to him and was at peace because Joseph continued to produce incredible results in all he did. Please don't be the person who is entrusted with something (big or small) and can't deliver. Not only is it embarrassing to you but also to the Kingdom. Going the extra mile is a biblical principle. It's always best to under promise and over deliver than over promise and under deliver.

It Attracts Everyone

Imagine a dark night with no stars, no moon in sight, and there is a distant, small light in a house in the woods. That light attracts everything from insects to animals. Think of the bugs that a lamp attracts on a dark night. From spiders to mosquitos to moths to lady bugs, you name it. That is how favor shines. It attracts everyone; those with good intentions and bad. Joseph's prosperity attracted Potiphar's wife. Mrs. Potiphar I'll call her in this book. Now I want us to look at her in a different light that will make us understand the power of favor.

Verse 6 Nuggets:

- He paid all the bills and took responsibility over every detail in running the household
- Potiphar had completely trusted Joseph with everything. He only managed his food
- His investments were entrusted to Joseph
- Joseph's opinion really mattered. When in a time, season, place or circumstance he should have been treated as a slave (no rights, no future, no voice, no freedom), he was treated as an equal (intellectual, a God send, a man, a leader, an influence, a businessman). See what God can do for you when he favors a life? Never let your circumstances dictate your reality (Prov. 3v5-6).
- If someone had a snap shot of Joseph's life at this particular moment of elevation (Gen 39v2-5) as we often do of one another, it's easy to see a smooth-sailing climb for him; it's very easy to say, why him? What's so special about Joseph? Why is he being singled out? We ask these kinds of questions, never knowing what someone has been through or where there they are headed. May we always be ready to rejoice when our neighbor rejoices, celebrate with them and mourn with them, when they mourn! Joseph was set in place to bring (physical) salvation from a drought for everyone around him, not just his family.
- This man had everything going on for him. Not only was he a successful business man, a God-fearing man, kind, prosperous, and respectable, he was handsome in looks and stature. There's always a story to the greener grass on the other side. For Joseph his was fertilized by the betrayal of a dysfunctional family. Enjoy your green!

Genesis 39v7-10

We need to understand what we are up against when dealing with supernatural favor. Mrs. Potiphar can easily be seen as a tramp or loose woman to have the audacity to seduce a young Hebrew slave whilst her husband is away working; to defy her marriage bed. Is she a tramp or does she have tramp-like tendencies? After multiple second looks at this story, I started to look at this woman in a very different light. In no way am I making excuses or making light or justifying her actions. Infidelity has ruined and scarred many relationships of not just the direct people involved, but also their families. It causes much pain that sometimes takes years to heal. Concerning Mrs. Potiphar, I am bringing out the story in a different light for a particular revelation.

At first it's beautiful. There are hardly any fights and when they do happen, apologies are abundant and readily shared. The excitement and thrill of married life still tickles their bellies and phrases like "us against the world" and "as long as we have each other" roll-off the tongue with ease. When Potiphar messes up, he quickly buys flowers or buys her jewels to apologize, as well as, giving a heartfelt apology. Expensive gifts and trinkets are flowing. As time passes, the sweet stomach butterflies of being in love disappear and turn into ulcers caused by the realities of a complicated world. There are demands and desires building that are stressful and require money. There are more hours at work. Extended families, of which you have married into, have real issues. Pressure and expenses of children or no children, demands of the house and status in society that require help to be sought are heavy. Slaves are a necessity and are cheap labor. So laziness and idleness settle in and the list goes on. Mrs. Potiphar got herself into trouble for many reasons. These are the same reasons that I see us ignoring today and landing us into lustful temptations of the flesh in marriage. Success has a great side to it, but also has a harsh side, that we have to be prepared for and guard against as much as we can. There will be those who are leeches and not interested in you, but what they can take from you. Beware of the Mrs. Potiphars in your life.

Points to consider:

1. Lustful society: it was not uncommon to sleep with slaves. Sex was a part of their worship to their pagan gods in their temples. Lust and adulterous sexual activity was part of their society.

2. Unlike the Proverbs 31 woman, Mrs. Potiphar had way too much unproductive time on her hands. She is the antithesis of the Proverbs 31 woman. She is idle, spoiled, not in charge of her house and not running it well with the servants to follow suit. She just lives there and enjoys the

perks. She is not living her purpose.

3. Power is attractive. Here is a beautiful, young man who is successful and running her household probably better than her husband did. Business is better than it ever was, the staff excels at their chores and their finances are at a rising surplus. Joseph has a way with people. He is authority, changes the atmosphere in a room and pulls the best out of people. He is responsible, hard-working and a man of power.

4. Her own marriage is in trouble. Whether forced to marry Potiphar or willingly doing so, the realities of life have hit this marriage pretty hard. Long work hours, bills, boredom ever increasing arguments, lack of communication, broken promises, differing growth experiences, busyness and the demands of life have set in. Potiphar, as captain of the guard, took care of the affairs of Pharaoh's house just as Joseph took care of his. Potiphar's job was very involving and demanding. Leaving Pharaoh to cater to different things, he concentrated on running his household. I'm sure there were times that he was gone all day and even all night depending on the demands that Pharaoh had.

Genesis 39:7a says: *"And it came to pass after these things that his master's wife cast her eyes upon Joseph..."*

Mrs. Potiphar did not pounce on Joseph the minute he was brought into the house. "After these things" implies that time had passed, maybe even a few years. That involves the time period of being bought and coming to the house and learning the ways and systems of the house. Numerous circumstances arose that involved Joseph's input, so his Godly character in word and deed was undoubtedly and undeniably distinguished. I'm sure the slave women and men were attracted to him, too. Time had to pass where Joseph was given projects in and outside of the house and he produced impressive, phenomenal results, so much so, that not only were other slaves noticing, he caught the eye of leadership (of Potiphar). Time had to pass where he was being watched for how he handled conflict, rebuke and instructions. Was he loving? How was he treating others? What about his level of respect, his loyalty and his speech, was it pretentious? All this was on display.

So the perfect scenario for an affair to blossom has been created. Thank God for his word that says in *1 Cor. 10v13: "No temptation has overtaken you except such as is common to man; but God is faithful, who will not allow you to be tempted beyond what you are able, but with the temptation will also make the way of escape, that you may be able to bear it."*

So to escape temptation we can:

a. Look for testimonies of those who have escaped the same temptations we go through.

b. Know that God is so faithful (keeper of his word) and will not allow you to be tempted more than you can bear (not to mistaken with burdens).

c. Know that God has already made a way of escape. Even if it isn't an easy way of escape, it is right there. For Joseph it was to RUN!

d. I know Joseph didn't have the option to but don't surround yourself with the temptation. Begin to have conversations with your Reuben, Simeon and Levi on how to operate.

e. Pray over your marriages and vigorously invest in making them echo God's perfect intent of marriage. Neglecting and taking a spouse often leads to breeding grounds for trouble. Mrs. Potiphar kind of trouble.

Chapter 7
The Power of Preparation
(How God prepares our gifts in the prisons of life)

I have come to appreciate the importance of preparation. I'm sure you've heard the phrase "it's all in the preparation." Yes, it is. If prep time is rushed or prolonged, or certain ingredients left out or too much added in, then the end products flawed, unprepared or unstable. Good preparation is either long, spread out over many, many years or it is short and unbearably intense. Whichever way, it is extremely important for the durability of the end product. No one wants something that looks great but breaks down easily, malfunctioning, or causes deathly side effects because it was rushed during preparation time. This is one of the causes of company recalls on products. Cutting corners to speed up production, or using cheaper materials to mass produce seems to be the way things are being done. Phones are only good for a year before glitches start popping up or they just don't work anymore.

This is the place that is very easy to despise because it looks contrary to the dream, vision or purpose. It's lonely, confusing, frustrating and humbling to be in preparation. More than ever, you have to stay motivated and keep pressing even when things are not looking up and disappointment becomes a part of life. Truly, it is a time to trust in the Lord with all your heart and lean not to your own understanding (Prov. 3v5) because the circumstances can be very depressing. But it is the perfect classroom for the gift or gifts God is sharpening in that season, to get you to the next level.

Imagine Joseph at 17 and all is going well. Even though he has disappointments such as malicious brothers, he has a promise from God about his future. His father was encouraging him about his future. His father even dressed him for success by making him the multi-colored coat, and honored him as overseer and supervisor of his brother's work. Believing he was destined for greatness was not a hard thing or impossible thing to embrace. The evidence was right there. Besides, they were living in Canaan, the Promised Land. To him it may have looked like they already arrived. Little did he know the training had only started! Training also includes testing. His father, mentoring him from his birth, began his training. His dreams initiated his call and Egypt birthed it.

We are called, then trained (preparation and testing), and then promoted. This is the cycle of life for the dreamer, going from glory to glory and faith to faith.

Genesis 40

I remember sharing many of these thoughts with my daddy; all the different revelations the Lord was giving me about the life of Joseph. His favorites were these I'm sharing with you in this section.

When we look at the dungeon, the natural eye sees a cold, dark, place of final judgment, which is condemning and miserable. It is the cold, dark, intense moments in our lives that produce our diamonds. That's how diamonds are made; from carbon deep, deep, in the earth and they undergo tremendous pressure and heat in darkness to be formed. The dungeon was the place strong enough to hold Joseph and position him for greater. With God on his life and prosperity in his life, Joseph could have blossomed anywhere in the world but his assignment was in Egypt. What Pharaoh saw before him was an undeniable, rare diamond (that didn't flaunt its value, manipulate to get ahead, beg nor coerce, steal to obtain more, nor cheapen its value to fit in) that he undoubtedly would polish to freely shine in his kingdom.

So much was happening in the dungeon that is applicable to our lives and we can use the rhema (revelation) to let our souls be comforted by what God is doing. He is working it all out for our good because He loves us, we love Him and have a relationship with Him. Jesus had 30 years of preparation. Moses had 40, Joshua, 40, David about 15 and so we must also have our share in the pool of preparation. We must have our wildernesses, training, preparation and testing times. We are not exempt from it. In fact, the greater you are to be used, the more intense your training will be. It's not Heaven being hard on you, but training you and preparing you. It is brutal and requires strength, grace and a tenacious spirit to go through preparation for greatness. It is not for the faint of heart. Be encouraged, though, that strength and wisdom come from the Lord. It is a love relationship because many walk away when it's rough and unbearable.

Lessons to learn from Joseph's dungeon experience (about 3- 10 years) that help us embrace ours:

a. Anytime you stand up for righteousness or holiness there will be earthly consequences to pay. There will be persecution, intense scorn, biased judgment and you will be looked down upon in the worst way possible. Joseph didn't end up in the dungeon because he did something wrong but because he did something right. He stood up for righteousness and was punished for it. Jesus warned us of these things and encourages us to not lose heart. He suffered the worst of it by going to the cross. He understands our pain all too well. Every time you choose to step away from the norm or clique or tradition and be unique, you will be punished with rejection, ridicule, isolation and persecution. Stand strong! It is a choice of holiness.

b. A place to break the hold of past hurts and a place of personal reflection. The dungeon that allows time to think on many things. It's a crossroads to either plan on turning a leaf or planning revenge. I believe Joseph chose this time to release bitterness, exercise forgiveness and pray for a second chance. I also think its gloomy nature allowed him to put "bad" into its proper prospective. The dungeon does that.

c. A place where the gifts are stirred up and sharpened and perfected. Joseph was transformed from a dreamer to a dream interpreter to a vision caster to a vision implementer to a world leader. The dream shows us where we are headed but not the details of journey and all that we have within to get there. The dungeon stirred an entrepreneur spirit in him and sharpened it to its highest degree.

d. Greatness is perfected in solitude; the dungeon was a perfect hiding place to develop Joseph away from the eyes of Satan or others who would have used him for what he had to share. There was so much in him and people would have taken advantage of greatness for their personal gain.

   • Because of love, God protects by hiding people for a season, to be later exposed as a force to be reckoned with (Moses, Jesus, Jacob, Eve).

- Know that in the hidden places, you will be overlooked no matter how anointed you are.
- Privacy is needed for perfection (Adam was put in a deep sleep during Eve's creation and formation)
- Character building – what's done in the dark comes to the light. Character being developed in the dark will show in the light. Train well!

e. A place where you learn to genuinely celebrate others and mourn when they mourn. Joseph was able to deliver great news to the butler and celebrate with him and soon coming victory despite his own victory was a mystery. He was truly disturbed by their downcast faces and was genuinely interested in encouraging them. You learn how to look out for others, even though your own situation isn't the greatest. There is nothing like having a friend to hold your hand when you're smiling and when you're crying.

Do not allow the dungeon to make you bitter and unpleasant. Instead make the dungeon a better place for others. That's the Joseph anointing flowing out of your heart. It takes Godly character to be that influential to make another's dungeon experience a more pleasant one. With it, we can help others find the love of God and be content in the prison state. Can you imagine how many people glorified God because of Joseph's pleasant attitude, love and concern for people? We are to shine wherever we are planted.

As your gifts are perfected, know that many will notice and desire its benefits. It is a time that your uniqueness of your gift is being recognized. (Gen. 40v16: and when the chief baker saw that the interpretation was good, he said unto Joseph, I also was in my dream and behold, I had three baskets on my head...)

In one season, offenses and dreams put him in the pit and in the dungeon they took him to the palace. The baker and cupbearer offended Pharaoh and all three had dreams. God uses the smallest insignificant this things of this world for His glory. What got us into a mess in one season gets us out the next. Nothing is impossible with God. That's why when offenses happen, look to God who is able to use them for His master plan. It is also a place where you learn about the power that you have to walk in loneliness and be content with that. Leaders don't usually fit in with a lot of people and the dungeon season is great time to learn to be at peace with that. Joseph the gifted foreigner, a slave and a prisoner is in charge of other prisoners, staff, and the guards. With every opportunity to escape or exercise tyranny he made the dungeon a place of ministry. Does your inner Joseph blossom wherever it is planted? Selah.

And finally allow it to be the place you learn the language of the culture of the people you are going to lead. Learning the mindsets of people, their likes and dislikes, how they treat the least among them, their food, their language, their ways of trade, their history, are great ways to understand people. And as a servant people will show you exactly who they are because servants are seen and not heard. Joseph was able to learn the language well and quickly. If you understand the language, you understand the people and the culture. (as a dignitary he would have been assigned an interpreter as in Gen. 42v23). Being servant –like teaches you to be slow to speak ad quicker to listen. You learn more by listening. Be encouraged knowing Jesus went through it too coming as a vulnerable baby and growing up knowing our ways. It allowed him to be touched by our infirmities as it would allow Joseph to see the injustices in Egypt.

Chapter 8
Elevation vs. Exposure
(Elevation + Exposure = Promotion)

I have often found myself praying for the Lord to elevate me and others because I understood it only from a physical sense and what I see and hear with my natural eyes and ears. Yet with God, elevation is transformation that happens in private. I had to learn to PRAY for PROMOTION. There is a difference between elevation and promotion. Elevation is the change in nature (change and structure, transformation in intellect, and mindset done in secret) whereas promotion is elevation plus exposure.

Elevation + Exposure = Promotion

Psalms 75v6: *"For promotion cometh neither from the east nor from the west, nor from the south, but God is judge; he putteth down one and setteth up another."*

You just came from reading about the dungeon – in the dungeon is where elevation happens. We can't have promotion without elevation, maybe from people (which will be short-lived). He loves you way too much to bring promotion to you unprepared. Elevation and preparation are seasons mentioned in the previous chapters that an individual must go through.

I am absolutely fascinated with how diamonds are made. As I mentioned earlier, they start up as carbon and after undergoing intense pressure and heat from the earth's core in total darkness, are elevated in form to diamonds. They are formed in the upper mantle between the earth's core and the earth's crust.

Diamonds are made in the upper mantle which is about (93.206 miles or 150 km) into the earth. A place of extreme pressure from the earth's crust and creation (mountains, etc.) and intense heat from the core; the upper crust is too deep in the earth to be mined. Scientists suspect that diamonds are pushed upward by vicious activity, therefore creating greater accessibility for us to mine diamonds closer to the earth's surface. Our equipment will only allow us to mine closer to the surface instead of layers deeper than that in the earth.

As the carbon atoms are joining to form a gem, elevation begins. It happens in the darkness when no one but God is watching. Likewise in the dark quiet moments of our lives, He is perfecting all that concerns us, stirring and perfecting His gifts in us. Underdeveloped gifts [diamonds] at a moment of exposure will not receive the same attention as a real diamond would. Allow patience to have her perfect work in you so your diamond(s) can be fully formed. The heat of the oven cooks the cake and the time makes sure it's cooked at the way through, not just on the outside. Don't fight staying in the oven and risk being pulled out too soon with a gooey center. (Gen. 41v1) *"And it came to pass at the end of two full years, that Pharaoh dreamed..."*

Joseph felt ready to be out of the dungeon in Chapter 40v14-15 as would we. No one wakes up hoping to live in filth, trials, and dungeons forever. But God made him go through two more complete years after he interpreted the dreams of Pharaoh's chief butler and chief baker. When God is promoting you, he makes sure only He gets the glory and that you are ready for it. He allowed the butler to forget Joseph so he could stay there longer for his transformation. Don't lose heart when you are forgotten, looked over and passed over for an open door. God is working it all out for His glory. Man may forget you, but God won't. He allows them to do so because he's making your promotion that much sweeter. It is working it out for your good because of your love and purpose.

Golden Nugget: Rejection is my friend ~ I forgive you for forgetting me, overlooking me and using me. I spoke of your freedom and you easily forgot mine. But I see now why you did. And I appreciate you. Had you spoken of it, I would have not had the classroom of the dungeon to sharpen the governor in me.

In elevation, greatness is developed and exercised so that it flows and operates as second nature. Joseph was an administrator and governor way before he stood before Pharaoh. Your calling is not just what you do. It is what you do because of who you are.

So then what is exposure?

Exposure is about bringing something to light, the showing and unveiling in public that what has been formed in secret. It requires vulnerability (free dictionary: "an act of subjecting or an instance of being subjected to an action or an influence) to the revelation of hidden things. Synonyms are; Uncover, revelation, disclosure, unveiling, unmasking, discovery, detection, denunciation, and condemnation. Meriam Webster dictionary defines it as "the condition of being presented to view or made known; the condition of being unprotected (like from bad weather); the condition of being subject to some effect or influence; disclosure of something secret; positioning with respect to (weather) influences or (compass) points.

It is the digging up of the diamond. A diamond is not a diamond because we polish it and cut it. It was always one in the ground (elevated). Joseph was elevated in the dungeon and was polished by Pharaoh (Gen. 41v14) and put on display. The very thing that got Joseph sold (dreams), got him out (dreams) (Gen. 41v1) out of prison. When God is involved, don't underestimate the power of your gift. The very thing you think nothing of is the very thing he will use for your promotion. Don't give up on or belittle what God has placed in your hand because of strenuous seasons in your life. Like the woman with the oil in 2 Kings 4, a little oil was miraculously used to pay off her debts, save her sons and create a family business they could live off of. Imagine if Joseph decided to never dream again, or interpret dreams, and chose to live bitter because of the trouble and heart ache he'd faced. He would have been unprepared for his Kairos moment (special divine moment in time) with destiny. As treasure in earthly vessels there is so much God has placed inside of us. Your trial is the process chosen to mine the gems in you.

Also don't let your season determine importance of all your gifts. My dad taught us that gifts are not forgotten but rather sometimes are seasonal. Some will go to the background already sharpened to allow others come to the spotlight to be sharpened. Just because they take a backseat, it doesn't mean they are non-existent. Joseph knew the power of a dream because it was what was keeping him alive and he never forgot it (Gen 42v9). Side note: God allows us to go through certain things so we can sympathize with others when they go through the same thing.

Exposure is the public recognition of the gem that you are: the unveiling, unmasking, discovery, the acknowledgement. It requires doing the right thing, being at the right place, at the right time with the right people. It is David before Goliath, Jesus at the Cana wedding, Jacob and Laban, and Daniel before Nebuchadnezzar. What you have gone through or birthed, elevation is now put on display. It is not forced, manipulated, planned or self- calculated, but desired, anticipated, and God-ordained. I love hustle-free moments of destiny. Only God sets up Kairos moments of exposure and no one can set them up like He does. Every detail is perfect, every moment strategically calculated, every individual precisely placed and each circumstance thoroughly calculated. He is truly a wonder.

Pharaoh is disturbed by those dreams because Pharaohs were considered gods and responsible for providing harvest and food for their people. This dream of the thin cows overpowering and eating the fat ones played heavily on his ego. He truly was desperate to know what was going on. God used that situation to expose, not only Joseph, but himself as the True and Only Lord of the harvest! The dream giver, interpretation giver, The Holy Spirit, The true God, Overseer, Provider, and One True God!!! Your moment of exposure is God's debut of his unveiling to the world as well. He gave the dreams to Pharaoh so God as the true deity could be revealed and also to fulfill to the dreams He gave to Joseph. What your Pharaoh is dreaming is lining up with your destiny and your dreams. Your calling is not insignificant. Your dreams are literally the answer to some body's nightmares. Our God is in control of everything. Your response is to trust Him with the details.

Several things must happen for exposure to happen in your life and we will look at Joseph for those principles:

a. Two complete full years passed before Pharaoh had the disturbing two dreams. Joseph would have been using his own strength and resources tirelessly and in an unwise manner to get out of the dungeon he thought didn't belong in. *1 Colossians1:9, "being filled with the knowledge of His will in all wisdom and spiritual understanding."* The ability to survive in the dungeon has a secret: the power of information. Being filled with the will of the knowledge of God (his plans, his intentions, his foresight, his purpose) having a plan brings peace and rest. Joseph coming out before the two years may have granted him freedom but not fulfillment. Standing before Pharaoh guaranteed him both of his God-given dreams. Let patience have her perfect work in your life. Those two years solidified his training as a vision implementer.

b. The Joseph anointing flourishes most where crisis and problems arise. God has raised you as a solution to a specific problem in the earth. That's why the enemy works tirelessly to ensure you don't see the authentic you. Detach yourself from conversations that have the sole purpose to complain and mention problems only. You are a problem solver. Guard your mind as one. Maybe you can't physically get into positions to get your voice heard for change, but you can pray. Prayer has more power than we think it has. Don't stop praying and be the change you want to see. Get to work!

c. ONE Joseph, ONE Pharaoh. Allow God to present you before your Pharaoh and his crisis or present him his crisis for you to solve in the power of God. Remember to not overwhelm yourself trying to do everything. I've found that just because I'm good at something doesn't mean it's the season for it or I'm the best candidate for the assignment. It's important to always check with the Holy Spirit if the task at hand is a good thing or a God thing.

d. Being at the right place at the right time. The dungeon was the right place for Joseph. Don't escape your dungeon because it's taking too long. God knows where you are, your address, situation and phone number. He'll come for you. He always does. He will meet you right where you are.

e. Operating in love today prevents burning important bridges. If Joseph had mistreated the chief butler and baker and not shared his gift, the butler would have not referenced Joseph later when Pharaoh needed his dreams interpreted. Don't live in bitterness because of what people have done to you. You don't always know whose presence you're in and who you are entertaining. Love helps us treat people well, no matter who they are and where we are. Had Joseph mistreated them, it would have taken more effort on Joseph's part to build the bridge to Pharaoh. Treat people well!

f. Let humility grow in your character in the dungeon, you'll need it when you stand before Pharaoh:
    *   Give glory to God for your gift(Gen 41v16, 25)
    *   Use your gift to bless others (Gen 41v28-36, especially v33)
    *   Don't toot your own horn (Gen 41v38,39)

Polish up on the skills and protocol expected in the palace. Learn or improve your communication (public speaking, etc), etiquette and decorum. Daniel, Shadrach, Meshach and Abednego together with the other captives were given

91

three years of scholarly training and palace protocol before they ever stood before King Nebuchadnezzar. Perfect your level of ability: plan, well, start well and finish well. While remembering that finishing what you started should also be done in a timely fashion, which takes discipline. Over the seven years of plenty Joseph faithfully saved 20% of the harvest for the famine ahead (Gen. 47v14, 20 and 23-26).

Respecting boundaries and guidelines is crucial for a leader [with the Joseph anointing]. God told Joshua and the children of Israel to possess the land he had for them but also gave the boundaries to not cross. A leader that has no boundaries is a dangerous one, subjecting his or herself to power they cannot handle. Joseph lived as disciplined leadership in Potiphar's house and in the dungeon so he could easily govern Egypt the same way.

g. Learn how to multi-task, work under pressure and learn to be responsible of more (Gen 41v39-50). A lot is assigned to Joseph almost overnight. He is governor and ruler over a whole nation. He's a newly-wed and soon to be a father. Each one of those demands much time. Multitasking is taught in the dungeon on how to handle many responsibilities at the same time. He was a great husband, a great father, great entrepreneur and great leader.

h. Learning to dream big makes you think big (41v49-57). Egypt stored so much grain that it was not able to be counted. A big dreamer plans big, so much that not only Egypt benefitted from the savings, but the whole world. It's not just about saving, but you making an impact on national, continental and global levels.

When all these elements were in place for Joseph, he was ready, at age 30, to have the stench of the dungeon be erased from his life and the effects of the past to be shaved off of him. He was able to walk into what God had destined him to be.

God wants you out of that situation and onto the path of destiny more than you do. Do you believe that? Isn't that just beautiful? So much that He hastily had Joseph removed from the dungeon and you, too, will be removed. He really does have great thoughts and plans concerning us (Jer. 29v11) and He dances over us (Zeph. 3v17). God has an appointed time for you. Rest in that promise today! As the master potter knows when the finished product of the clay is complete and removes it off the wheel, so does he know your spinning time on the wheel. We now have the grace of Jesus Christ to keep us going through those moments when we feel we can't go on. Know that Jesus is a friend that sticks closer than a brother and will not leave you, but is faithful to complete the good work He started in you and faithful to keep His promises and covenant with you (Phil.1v6). The One who gave Joseph his dreams and brought them to pass, will do the same for you. Just stay centered in him. When a clay pot is being made, the most crucial part of the process is called 'centering' the clay in the middle of the wheel so the potter doesn't fight with it.

I love big impossible dreams. They remind me of how big my God is. All I have to be is me and God will work it out all the impossible details. I have learned to do my part and let God do His. His word is a lamp unto my feet and light unto my path (Ps.119:105); the good steps of a righteous man are ordered by the Lord (Ps.37:23).

Golden Nugget: Promotion 101~ Carbon becomes a diamond in the dark (ELEVATION). A mined, polished (EXPOSURE) and cut diamond on display is PROMOTION (elevation plus exposure). PRAY for PROMOTION which only comes from God.

Chapter 9
Your Inner Jacob

Gen.42v1-3: "Now when Jacob saw that there was corn in Egypt, Jacob said unto his sons, why do ye look upon one another? And he said, Behold I have heard that there is corn in Egypt. Get you down hither and buy for us from thence; that we may live and not die. And Joseph's ten brothers went down to buy corn in Egypt."

One of my favorite topics (other than identity in Jesus Christ) is one fulfilling their assignment and core purpose with divine strategy. Strategy fascinates me, excites and entices me. I find it so valuable and an essential ingredient to success. You can have all ducks in a row but if strategy isn't implemented, well then, the ducks will stay in line with nowhere to go. A brilliant purpose remains stagnant when the right strategy isn't applied.

Their purpose was to live and be prosperous in Canaan, but a famine (death, dryness, unfruitfulness, lack) fell upon the land of plenty. It had been their place of abundance, wealth, health, life and prosperity. They were in the place of promise already, but death attacked. Jacob represents and symbolizes the kind of person we must become in order for Israel to shine to its capacity. Jacob shows us how to keep pressing in the tight places, in the difficult phases and in the impossible climates of life.

At one point things are flourishing and it is business as usual, there's plenty of harvest, the wells are full water, the flocks are multiplying and the promised land of Canaan is the land flowing with milk and honey. But just like that, death in form of a famine begins to creep in month after month, and stays year and year. Does that sound familiar to you? Where lack suddenly crept in and stayed long enough it became the norm?

Unaware of the information Joseph had about the famine, Jacob and his sons were living in this state prayerfully hoping each month was the end of the worst of it. Similarly as each month comes by, you stand on the word of God that his promises are yes and amen, that your breakthrough is near and that He will provide. You've been fasting, praying, tithing, serving, praising, believing, hoping and declaring but the famine or lack is only getting worse. You're left tired, defeated and unproductive, stuck in a status quo and in a rut of uncertainty and hopelessness. Everything you have tried for increase that worked in the past is not working now and like Pharaoh's dream, the lean cows have eaten up the fattened ones and there is no proof that they ever existed. There is no proof that you once had much, once had great health, or once was happily married… LACK is the only reality of everything in your possession. The sick, lean cows devoured the fat cows. Joseph interpreted in 41v30,31, *"And there shall arise after them seven years of famine; and all the plenty shall be forgotten in the land of Egypt; and the famine shall consume the land; and the plenty shall not be known in the land by reason of that famine following; for it shall be very grievous."* Life is getting harder each minute. Your worst situation has now become your best with no knowledge of when the vicious cycle will end. You were once able to save and store up, but now you live paycheck to paycheck and before long bills are piling up and you're living on future paychecks, eventually, on nothing. The famine is becoming severe.

Genesis 42:1 ~ "Now Jacob saw that there was grain in Egypt, and Jacob said to his sons, "Why are you staring at one another?" He said, "Behold, I have heard that there is grain in Egypt; go down there and buy some for us from that place, so that we may live and not die."...
Jacob teaches us that there comes a time where God presents us with the opportunity to choose life or death; to choose if we will become victims of circumstances or victors over the famine-stricken situations. It's time for your Jacob to speak to self (Reuben, Simeon, Levi, Judah, Zebulun, Issachar, Dan, Gad, Naphtali, and Asher) that it's time for change, time to choose life and GO WHERE the provision is. It doesn't always physically mean to relocate but to stop looking at yourself for answers that you are not able to produce. Go where the

answers currently are. Go where others are thriving despite facing the same famine attacking you. So here are some practical ways to do that:

a. Change your mind set to embrace that there are other ways of doing things. Don't hold onto what's not working for sake of security: "Sticking to the same old-same old, this is how we've done this for years and this is what we'll do it forever" mentality. Like a hamster on its wheel, running tirelessly but not going anywhere. Listen to your inner Jacob prompting you to step out of the box and enter into the greatness God has for you. It will require doing something new, maybe going somewhere new and meeting new people. It's like the Zambian proverb my mom taught us "that if you don't travel, you will think your mom is the best cook in the world."

b. Don't look for answers from people who are in the same mess you are in. It's the message of the blind leading the blind. That's why Jacob said, why do you look on each other? Your resources together are limited so look elsewhere. Or even within yourself there are no solutions, so glean from a voice that has been where you are trying to go.

c. Sometimes we find ourselves waiting on God, when God is waiting on us. I do believe there are seasons where we are to be completely still and do what we need to do and wait on the Lord to work things out for us. Wilderness experiences where God's provision of manna sustains us till he opens other doors for us. What often happens, like the children of Israel in the wilderness, is we adapt to the wilderness and either delay the crossover, or never get the chance to. Let Jacob speak to your Issachar to sharpen his awareness of the seasons and times you are in. Know when a season is starting and when it is over. That powerful statement right there will save you many tears, bad decisions and frustration when you live by it. Joseph said it was a concluded matter that the famine would last seven years. *(Amos 3v7: "surely the Lord God will do nothing but He revealeth His secret unto His servants the prophets.")*. Allow patience to train your Issachar how to detect seasons and work the grace God supplies to survive the set years of the famine, or situation. Because there is a time for everything and God gives the grace needed for that season.

d. Jacob did not send one son to Egypt, he sent ten. There are many biblical meanings of the number ten but I want to focus on one here. Ten symbolizes God's creative power. He sent ten in search of new beginnings to create new and bring back sustenance for life (food) where death (famine) was reigning. Develop and surround yourself with a strong team of people with different gifts, talents and qualifications to help you (Jacob) achieve the vision. They don't have to be in your inner circle but, they must embrace your vision.

That shows that the Jacob mentality or Jacob anointing is important in our lives in order for us to transform into Israel. Jacob is the bud that blooms into Israel. One is created and the other is formed (Isaiah 43:1). Jacob was an amazing man that we can learn a lot from. Prior to the story of his sons, Jacob from his birth on, he was constantly being prepared for his name change:

a. Jacob was a fighter for greater: Gen. 25v31 ~ The birthright and it's privileges belonged to the first born (Esau, his older twin brother) but Jacob didn't care because the greatness in him (not greed) cried out for more. He seized the opportunity when he was presented it. I believe long before "the soup for birthright" situation he saw his brother's flippant behavior towards his birthright and waited for the right moment to claim it for himself. Opportunity doesn't change you, like money and power, it brings out what is already inside of you. .

b. Jacob was a mentor for the peculiar: (Gen. 25v28) Jacob was loved dearly and mentored by his mother, Rebekah. She had stronger vision (Isaac's eyes were dim) and was able to see the greatness in Jacob and guided him in the direction of receiving the first born blessing. She knew where Jacob needed to get the blessing to unlock the unfamiliar greatness in him and she positioned him for it. Likewise he saw something peculiar in Joseph and positioned him to go ahead of his brothers, conquer the dungeon and save his family.

c. Jacob was a man of personal God encounters: encounters where God spoke with him and changed his life (they had relationship). Whether in visions (Gen. 28v12-22) or physical encounters (32v1-24; 35v9-15), Jacob was a man deeply transformed and affected by the presence of God. The key ingredient in your transformation is your relationship with God. Desire God encounters because they will change your life forever. Jacob wrestled with God and would not let go until God blessed him. It was then that his name was changed, calling redefined and his walk changed forever. Let the Jacob in you have a personal real and substantial relationship with God the Father, The Son and Holy Spirit.

d. He is a man of purpose and promise (Gen. 28v15). This was my father's favorite verse. He taught me that when you know your purpose, you also hold your promise that life is your portion. God makes a promise to him that Jacob will not die until the purpose is fulfilled. That's how he knew that the famine would not kill them because his entire purpose has not been fulfilled. When you find your purpose you have the flag of life's longevity to wave in the face of death when it comes knocking.

e. The Uncle Labans in our lives: Jacob needed to face the ultimate trickster to burn out he trickster in him. Just like David, needed Saul to burn the Saul in him. Don't despise the Labans that come to remove the ugly in you Jacob. It's all part of the metamorphosis. Some seasons are so uncomfortable but they are extremely important. You need people that are an unpleasant version of you to kill the germinating seed of unpleasantness in you. Uncle Laban will make you think twice before you trick anyone else.

f. He has been through very difficult lows and tremendous highs and still loves God. I need a mentor with testimony, who's been through the fire, storms, earthquakes and wind (Like Elijah was for Elisha in 1kings 19). I don't want someone who just made it through the fire, got scared, played it safe and now has chip on their shoulder (47v9) but a person who came out with so much testimony. I want someone full of wisdom and love for the Lord, someone who lives by the fruit of the Holy Spirit!

g. A man of integrity: Integrity will do the right thing even if it pains him. He was deceived to marry Leah and worked for another seven years for Rachel. He didn't divorce Leah. You can't teach integrity if you personally don't live by it. He had every right to get even with Laban, but served him faithfully for another seven and then some (and left when Joseph was born). True, he was not always a loving husband to Leah and he clearly favored Rachel more but he never abandoned Leah. He provided for Leah and took care of her and their children.

h. A Jacob is a peace maker. He wants peace, so he creates it. There's a proverb in my mother tongue (Bemba) which translates "he who wants peace creates the peace." Also, Matthew 5v9 reads; *"blessed are the peace makers for they shall be called sons of God."* He didn't stay to fight with Esau and neither did he fight with Laban. He made peace with both men and even made amends with Prince Shechem over his daughter Dinah. He is a man of greatness ruled by the peace in his heart.

i. He wrestled with God and never let go, until God blessed him. Don't wrestle with people, who have finite power, to make drastic changes in your life. In other words put your energy into prayer and divine strategies with God for the transformational change you desperately desire. Jabez (whose name means sorrow) didn't fight with mother about his name but went to God in prayer and asked for the miracle to have his life changed despite the misfortune of his name. Where are you spending your energy and resources in order to create change?

Chapter 10
Ability and Character

"Ability takes you to the top and character keeps you there."

¬Apostle Ronald Chapoloko Sr.

his motto is one my siblings and I have cherished for years. As mentioned earlier it is a golden nugget our daddy taught us as we began to experience life's iron sharpening seasons. The pressure would be so unbearable sometimes I thought I'd never make it but I held onto this truth that guaranteed I was coming out refined and polished on this other side. That my survival at the top was determined secure by my character development rather than by my comfort. The great testimony and example of him and my lovely mother was inspiring: they declared it, lived it and instilled it in us. So I knew without a shadow of a doubt we were destined to make it too.

The first part of this book dealt with preparation, elevation, exposure, and showing how preparation is character building. So in this chapter I what to focus on what [Godly] character is and it's characteristics that keep you soaring as the eagle that you are. I heard a quote that blends beautifully with my dad's motto and so fitting for this chapter: "We know that what's in you must sustain you at the altitude you ascend to" – Christine Cane.

So what is in us?

      a.   The Holy Spirit works to develop the seed of salvation planted in us to bear fruit ~The fruit of the Spirit: *"But the fruit of the Spirit is love, joy, peace, longsuffering (patience), gentleness, goodness, faith, meekness, temperance (self-control)..."* – Galatians 5v22-23. It is the fruit that is the evidence of maturity and soundness of mind. It is the anchoring force of the Holy Spirit that maintains stability in our lives when everything around us is changing. It shields the perception of our identity from being tarnished when our surroundings are always so eager to redefine us. It is the sound mind of the Holy Ghost that rests in the heart of individual to be who they are in Christ no matter where they are in life. You've heard it said that new levels bring different devils, new challenges and new pressures. The fruit of the Spirit also prevents us from being defeated, double minded and tossed to and fro by the new enemies we face. It causes us to the handle the pressures at any level and dimension. The fruit of the Spirit is about "being"; the human "being" loving, patient, kind, meek, etc. Not forced but a naturally flowing temperament of *love, joy, peace, patience, gentleness, goodness, faith, meekness, self-control.*

b. Dominion and leadership: You were created to be the head and not tail, to be in dominion and leadership in the earth. That for whatever responsibilities are placed in your hands, excellence, productivity, and prosperity are your portion. Like the parable of the talents, each person's talent share is different but fruitfulness was expected all across the board. Stewardship in excellence over anything placed in your hand shows a lot about your character. Joseph whether a slave in Potiphar's house, overseer in the dungeon, governor over Egypt or leader of the world's food industry, worked diligently and in prosperity, always producing impeccable results with a good attitude. Let the Joseph in you bloom in leadership wherever you are planted.

c. Loyalty: The value of keeping our word is something society is losing very quickly. In previous times, one's word meant everything. Your yes was a yes and your no a no. Merriam-Webster describes loyalty as "a feeling of strong support for someone or something." In order to show loyalty, we must display it out through word and deed. Let the Naphtali (speech and tongue) in you arise as a loyal and faithful word spoken. Let your yes be yes and no be no (Matt 5:37 & James 5:12).

d. Compassion: One of the things I loved about Jesus was His compassionate heart. He came with the authority and power of Heaven, the King of Kings with glory and majesty in His hands. He is the captain of the Lord's army and with one word commands the angels to do his will. Yet, He was moved with compassion for people; never inconvenienced and always

101

eager to enrich the lives of others. He healed, delivered, and ministered to them, not because His gift needed an outlet, but because His compassion for people moved Him to operate in his greatness. Godly character is being moved by compassion and flowing in our gifts and callings to bless people. It is not so much about using our gifts because of the need to express oneself but rather expressing oneself because there is a need. When we exercise the former instead of the latter it positions excessive convenience (which is the enemy of compassion) to rule.

e. Restorer/Redeemer: what you do with your platform of promotion will expose the soundness of your character. Will your promotion be used solely for personal gain, revenge and as a soap box? Or will you allow your inner Joseph to nourish the Israel in you and others? Joseph was able to restore and nourish his father's household and many other lives. He had every chance and opportunity to mistreat his brothers, but saw that it was the Lord who sent him to Egypt (the way He chose to) to prepare him to nourish and preserve his brothers (Israel). We must have character that restores people, restores relationships, repairs broken systems, redeems lost ones and restores life; one that builds for the Kingdom of Heaven.

f. Excellence: It's not just about getting the job done, but also how we get it done. Don't just show up. Show up to excel. Show up to win. Show up to make to a difference. Mediocrity, sadly, is becoming the new excellence. It's creeping into our society in very sly ways. Take for example in sports for children, it used to be that you had to practice, train, and work hard but these days, they are given trophies for showing up. I understand that we don't want to hurt their feelings, but what we are teaching them in the long run about the requirements of excellence is what's more important. They will expect rewards for doing little, and struggle in a world that does not function like that. Living to their full potential will be a struggle because of the seed of mediocrity planted in them.

g. Wisdom: If the Lord used wisdom to lay the foundations of the earth, then we cannot remove it from the equation for Godly character. We MUST operate and live in the wisdom of God. In the simplest of terms, wisdom is the ability to skillfully use and understand the knowledge you obtain on all matters. Knowledge is power but how you use power is wisdom. Wisdom works hand in hand with love where love serves as the fuel (gas/petrol) to the vehicle of wisdom. Let your inner Dan (wisdom) rise up tall and strong.

The spirit of excellence must be evident in our lives as it was clearly seen in Daniel. The willingness to be set apart whilst purposing in our hearts to be used for the Lord's glory. To be able to treat others well in the process, speaking the truth in love and respecting the leadership God places over us. To live the life that produces results from what we set ourselves aside to do. Are all components of the spirit of excellence; Godly character is this very thing.

Chapter 11
Your 42ⁿᵈ Chapter
(When God writes the story)

s I was writing this book, I was also working on its devotional. This chapter was inspired by one of the devotional entries I was writing. I knew I needed to write more on the revelation the Lord was giving me. It blessed me so much that I knew I needed to share what I was receiving.

If we could see the whole picture, I think we'd treat each other very differently. On this side of eternity, our minds are not able to handle that amount of knowledge. But once we are in glory and reigning with Jesus, 1 Corinthians 13, states that we know in part now, but one day will know as we are known. FULLY! We will know fully! He shows us where to step as a lamp unto our feet and also what to walk towards, as a light unto our path. We can't handle the entire reality of life thrown at us at the same time and I appreciate God's love to take that into consideration. It would take away trust, the thrill of life, exciting moments and, abilities to learn if all was revealed right away.

Solomon lived a life of wisdom and understanding (great things) and saw it all and called it vanity. His exposure to great volumes of wisdom took away the thrill of what he thought was life. There are some realities that are very difficult to handle but as they come God graces us for them: the death of a loved one, job loss in bad economy, divorce, betrayal, abuse, sickness, etc. Many times the knowledge of these is not always revealed at the beginning of the journey because it would discourage us from moving forward. In Genesis, God saw it best to have Adam in a deep sleep when he was making Eve. You know our nature. Adam would have tried help, suggesting and interfering with Eve's first encounter with God. [Ladies, let a man affirm what God has already told you in secret.] With our limited knowledge in mind, we must be careful not to judge (condemn or rule out as definite) a person's circumstances or our own based on a season of their life. They stripped Joseph of the outer manifestation of what was inside, as was shared in chapter three. Despite his cries of anguish, they enjoyed their bread, their substance, their increase, in earshot (and eyesight) of their brother's pain. Their disdain for their brother was based on limited information provided in that particular season of their lives. Let their actions be a mirror of what is in our sinful nature. Sometimes even the most anointed people can cause harm to others who are in the pit season of their lives. Like Joseph's brothers they put down others to feel better about themselves because it takes the attention off of their shortcomings. Despite these attacks Joseph, you will survive. You will live past this and live to forgive and nourish the ones that slander you. You will succeed Joseph, because you are a fighter. You will live past the PIT.

I want to encourage the Joseph in you to press on despite the negative critiquing and gossip sessions held in your honor. Collectively the gossiping tongues seem to triumph but the Lord has the final say. Blinded by their false sense of victory, they indulge in their bread, in their sustenance, their provision, their norm; and, for a season, it looks like they have won. They write you off and place you in a box marked for slavery, damaged goods and useless dreamer. They never again expect anything great from you because they have killed your dream, so to speak. Chapter 37 tells us that it is not the end of the story and their victory is short-lived. The author keeps writing and we keep reading. Because of our faithful God, there is a chapter 42.

Genesis 37v23-25 and 42v5-11:

In Chapter 42, we see that the tables have started to turn and in verse nine, we see Jacob advising his sons to not accept death and keep pressing forward to choose life. The bread is done. There are no more jobs to bring in sufficient income, not enough money, no vacations and the famine has brought death, a sore death. There was nothing to show for their previous victories and abundance. It was completely gone and done away with. The famine was so sore that it looked like there were never, ever seven years of plenty. Chapter 42 is God's chapter demanding recompense. The very men who got so insanely mad at their brother for sharing his dreams couldn't get to the ground fast enough before him in their time of need. Granted, they didn't know him but Joseph's dreams had been fulfilled. The same ones that spoke harshly to him when Joseph shared his dreams, called him lord and master when their bread was taken away. They described themselves now as his servants and not enemies. My God, when God polishes you, even those closest to you will not recognize you. Now that is what I call a makeover or transformation! Allow God to polish you in the pressure and in the fire. You are coming out victorious and like a polished diamond. Every tongue that laughed at you, insulted you and put you down will be humbled in the chapter 42 of your story; with what God is about to reveal in your life.

This should comfort you that when people misunderstand you and look down on you, it is God your Redeemer and Recompense that is the lifter of your head. Hold your peace that God knows how to show off in your life. Having connection with the Holy Spirit directing and bridling your tongue is a necessity. Seek His counsel about when to speak and when to be silent because our flesh can very easily kick in thinking we are speaking truth and letting it be known about who we are. Know that when God fights your battles, He fights to win and always does. The right conditions will cause people to be humbled and see you as God sees you and show you the respect you deserve. Sometimes, all we desire from people is respect. We may not be part of their norm, but desire respect regardless, knowing that God is leading our lives.

V9a: *"and Joseph remembered his dreams which he dreamed of them…"*

First point to consider: Gen. 37v9; sheaves represent a time of harvest and are used to make flour for bread. Only Joseph's harvest stood tall above the rest. The brother's harvest was nothing in comparison to Joseph's harvest. Out of his harvest, his father's household would be blessed. Your hater's bread might be in abundance now, but love them enough today to be able to sustain them one day when your harvest will be greater. Truly, humility must come with dream fulfillment because what God gives us has the purpose of edifying others as well. The abundance we are given is to bless and sustain others and, yes, including the undesirable. [Don't despise your hater, they helped sharpen your character… and don't be so quick to not love haters, to someone, somewhere YOU once hated on them.] Joseph was being used by God to provide for his people. He was the one God appointed and chose to bless them and honor his covenant to Abraham. Harvest is the multiplied product of what you have sown.

We judge by what others are doing or not doing instead of looking to see what seeds are they have sown. Sowing into heavenly store houses has great reaping benefits here on earth. Joseph's promotion was to oversee a harvest of great magnitude and its seeds were not only tangible but intangible. The seven years of plenty involved tangible seeds and the 30 years of preparation were the intangible seeds.

They crucified Jesus because they didn't like the packaging he came in. That's the same reason they are crucifying you. Walk away and keep pressing toward the mark of the high calling. God will use whomever He chooses and desires and has appointed. The clay cannot say to the Potter," why are you using me or that one"? It seemed to them that Joseph was already favored by their father therefore his big dreams from God irritated them. It wasn't up to them. God had already chosen his leader.

We use our human understanding to try to make sense of divine things. Prov. 3v5&6 and Col. 1v9 strongly encourage us to not lean on our own way of looking at things, but rather to see things from a spiritual standpoint and perspective. We cheapen the understanding of the will of God because of the packaging God uses to enlighten us such as dreams, thoughts, visions, ideas, our conscious, Jesus, and regular people. We don't like the packaging, so we reject the message. Prov. 8 says that wisdom is screaming loud in the streets. Embrace it, use it, cherish it for it is better than gold.

When you doubt the arrival of your Chapter 42 remember those who have gone before you and how God wrote it for them. Joseph's forefathers had thrived in famines and God had shown his faithfulness. And so God was going to give him his defining moment to see the faithfulness of God in a massive dry place.

Another point to take into consideration is Dream #2 (Gen. 37v9) concerning the stars, moon and sun. There is so much commentary on what this second dream meant. From the sun being Jacob, the moon being his Rachel or Leah and the eleven starts his brothers to the sun representing kings and the moon the church and the stars idol gods. I know God to be a multifaceted God with so many beautiful sides to his character and nature. I believe that even the dreams and visions He gives can have several messages, but I also love that He gave Joseph confirmation in this second dream to personally prepare him for the magnitude of his promotions.

Rightfully so Jacob should not have rebuked him, but rather further told him (with such big a dream) the bigger or grander the dream the harder the preparation. The moon and sun are symbols God uses to tell time and seasons. Throughout the Word, He tells what their various appearances will proclaim certain significant times. Day and night are determined by them. Shapes and shades of the moon determined feasts that were to later be observed. Throughout Revelation, the timing of certain events are heralded by the positioning and colors of the sun and moon. Although I am not a believer in Zodiac signs for direction in purpose [Astrology], I do believe that God placed messages in the stars and moons [Astronomy] as signs of seasons and times. These celestial beings all glorify God and He uses them to tell us about the seasons He has set in the earth. The bowing of these celestial beings could be based on the time period that God was giving Joseph, a clue of when he would be in power living out his dreams.

Other points about God's chapter 42

v13: *"And they said, thy servants are twelve brothers, the sons of one man in the land of Canaan; and behold the youngest is this day with our father and one is not."*

a. They had so thought little of their brother and presumed him too weak to survive slavery and therefore, presumed him dead. With slaves often sold and resold all over the world, the last place they expected to see Joseph was Egypt. It's clear when they arrived there, they were not expecting him to be alive, or they would have said it to this stranger they paid homage to. People write us off so badly and conclude that nothing good can come out of us. [What good can come out of Nazareth? Was asked concerning Jesus?] Little do they know that a life in the hands of God can shine like the sun! Truly, no mind, ear, nor eye has seen what God is able to do with you, but you can have a glimpse of it through the Spirit. That's why you can't be discouraged if not everyone or anybody (like in Joseph's case) doesn't fully understand your dreams. Keep dreaming and planning to fulfill them.

b. When God gives makeovers, they are so phenomenal that even those closest to you will not recognize you, as I mentioned before. Joseph had become the symbol of strength, poise, royalty and power. It never entered their minds that this was their brother. Even his speech was different (v23) and could speak the different tongue of his new place; he spoke the language of abundance, the language of destiny. Those that thought they had you all figured out will be doing a reevaluation of you as God has made some drastic changes for the better in your life.

Though they consider Joseph dead they still consider him their brother, not a dreamer or a pest as they once did, but a son of Jacob, their brother. They count themselves as 12 for the first time because a change over a period of 20 years has taken place in their hearts too. They had recognized their faults and how they wronged their brother. Joseph was their blood no matter what they had disliked or loathed about him. At the end of it all, family is family. Give people the time to come to the place where they realize and accept you as God made you and called you. The brothers started to see themselves as a unit, 12 sons of one man, children or denominations of one God, different parts of the body, but one head. It's important for us as believers to see past our differences (including convictions) and acknowledge our similarities and that we are of one God (1 Corinthians 12).

Another point to consider is from v17-26: You have become powerful. How will you use your platform? Settle that in your heart today. That's character! One of the ways to see how insecure someone is to see what they do with power. Joseph, by testing his brothers isn't insecure, but rather checking the quality of their hearts and if any change has been made. When you enter the place of destiny of being reunited with your dream, all things must be in order and in check with where your dream is. Your promise is now "calling the shots", not your feelings, flesh, intellect, etc. They have been put in check (prison v17) to show it is now time for the promise to come forth. Nothing will hold it back. Israel must function as 12, with Judah (praise) as the leader and the promise (Joseph) with the double portion. Israel, your dream is being perfected behind the scenes.

- v24; Simeon is the most wicked of his brothers because he represents the flesh of which the Bible says there is nothing good. Display to your feelings, praise, spirit man, wisdom, tongue, instinct, health, finances, warrior [His brothers] the arrest of flesh (Reuben) and that in this season, it has no power at all. In our lives as Christians, our flesh must always be silenced, daily we are to crucify it and render it powerless. Especially in our moment of greatness, it must be thrown in the pit to be shown who is really in control.

- You see your own feelings for what they really are (v22), unstable. As the oldest, Reuben should have taken responsibility and taken the blame for entertaining his brothers' idea to kill Joseph. He truly wanted to rescue him but he didn't act upon it. He played with fire and got burned. This is why the birthright was taken from him. He was unstable and irresponsible with his privileges. He didn't know his own strength (his father called him the beginning of his strength 49v3, power, might and excellence). He had a twisted view of this and he abused it and lost his birthright and leadership. A good leader knows the buck stops at him or her. Reuben didn't assume responsibility, but blamed his brothers even after all those years. I now understand why my parents always looked at me when my younger siblings were getting into trouble. I was asked why I, the oldest, let this happen. Reuben, as the leader where were you then and why didn't you stop this from happening? His power, might and excellence had the ability to prevent it, but he didn't use it. Reuben, your feelings are unstable. Don't make life changing decisions in this place of abundance and destiny.

- v25; Joseph, used his power, instead, to bless others, especially those that had hurt him because he knew they were one. They had a purpose to serve in his promotion. This is not the time to get even, but a time to live our purpose:
  - They got back their money.
  - They received nourishment to survive the famine that would have killed Israel and embarrassed God as their covenant provider.
  - They got more than they asked for, provision for the trip because God blesses above and beyond what we ask, think and imagine (Eph. 3v20)
  - It's like Esther, brought to the palace for such a time as this; brought here to serve a specific purpose in the kingdom of God and all things shall be added unto you (Esther 4v14 and Matt. 6v33)

Chapter 12
The Power of Praise

e must never underestimate [or cease in learning] the power of praise. As long as we live, we must allow the Lord to perfect this in us. It is what we were created to do; for our lives to be a praise and worship song to God. Everything we do, whether in common sense, ordinary, or spectacular, our lives are to give glory to God.

Gen. 29v35: *"And she conceived again, and bare a son; and she said now I will praise the Lord: therefore she called his name Judah; and left bearing."*

Leah's first three sons were named and birthed to please Jacob. We feel that if we first try hard enough, study hard enough, behave better, prophesy more, etc., people will accept and love us more. But like Leah, there's that moment of reckoning where we realize our lives are praise dance for an audience of ONE: THE GREAT I AM, ELOHIM, and God ALMIGHTY.

Leah birthed [and blessed] her fourth son from a place of praise, and called him Judah, because she finally realized no matter how mistreated she was her true happiness came from the Lord, the real object of her affection. Praise changed her life. It changed her mind set and the atmosphere in her home. Leah (who was not a beautiful as her sister Rachel) represents the areas we have that are not as desirable as the Rachel (gifts, splendor) in us; they are those areas we want to hide and we are ashamed of. Leah is trapped in a vicious triangle of injustice: her father's treachery, her husband's unkindness and her sister's mockery. The voice of her pain is silenced by her insecurities of insignificance, being undesirable, and the lack of options. The Leah in us has a silent scream that no one hears but the Lord. So he gives her the opportunity to speak by allowing her to birth out what is in her. She begins to speak with the hopes to be desired by her husband but soon learns her voice was made to glorify God and names her son Judah. May you discover the same purpose for the voice of your life!

Golden Nugget: Rejection is my friend ~ Thank you rejection for teaching me true worship. I birthed for people what I thought would make me acceptable to them but you have taught me to birth fruit for an audience of one. The ONE who has already accepted me!!!

1 Chronicles 5v2: For Judah prevailed above his brethren and of him came the chief ruler; but the birthright was Joseph's.

Genesis 49v8-12: Judah, you are he whom your brothers shall praise; Your hand shall be on the neck of your enemies; Your father's children shall bow down before you. ⁹ Judah is a lion's whelp; From the prey, my son, you have gone up. He bows down, he lies down as a lion; And as a lion, who shall rouse him? ¹⁰ The scepter shall not depart from Judah, Nor a lawgiver from between his feet, Until Shiloh comes; And to Him shall be the obedience of the people. ¹¹ Binding his donkey to the vine, And his donkey's colt to the choice vine, He washed his garments in wine, And his clothes in the blood of grapes. ¹² His eyes are darker than wine, and his teeth whiter than milk.

In this chapter, we look further at the maturity and character development of Judah and why he was raised up as the leader of his brothers. We first hear him speaking in Genesis 39 when he saves Joseph from being killed by his brothers and ten chapters later (over 20 years later) he is given the title as the first born of Israel. While Joseph was being perfected in Egypt, Judah was maturing in Canaan. As I mentioned earlier, it's not only about your dream coming to pass, it's about your whole being (Israel) maturing to be sustained by your dream. Trust that your dream is not forgotten but rather regard its silence as the season your spirit man/praise is developing into the leader it is. When the armies of the Lord were sent out to battle Judah was always first in line (then Issachar and Zebulan) because praise is powerful, chain breaking, wall crushing and atmosphere changing. Your vision is tarrying to strengthen the ultimate warrior in you.

Golden Nugget: The Power of Worship ~ The SHOUT of praise at Jericho was the first war the children of Israel won in the promised to show them that praise is their greatest weapon and a first fruit offering to the Lord!!!

Let's pick up the story at Genesis 43 where Jacob is unmovable on his decision to release Benjamin to his brothers at the governor's (Joseph's) request, as incentive for Simeon to be released. The famine had gotten worse and the corn from Egypt from the previous trip ran out and Jacob is in conversation with his sons about returning to Egypt for more food. But the terms for more still stood, Benjamin had to accompany his brothers. Mourning the loss of Joseph and imprisonment of Simeon, Jacob was understandably struggling with the conditions. Reuben, as I further explain in Chapter 15, is proving himself to be a dysfunctional leader with his poor reasoning and lack of foresight to their future. In Gen. 42v37-38, he offers the lives of his sons if he is unable to return with Benjamin. Jacob denies this offer for three reasons;

1. The word of a leader, who is willing to destroy today what is meant for the future (his two sons) over food, is not to be trusted. Jacob saw Esau in his son. Esau lost his birthright over a bowl of soup and his son was heading down the same path.

2. Jacob had suffered enough loss over the years. Those dear to him had died or been taken away and the thought of losing another child, disheartened him.

3. The word of a leader, who doesn't sympathize with people, is not to be trusted. Wisdom teaches when to speak, act or wait. Reuben is unable to see the pain his father is in even after all these years all because he has a hunger to satisfy. Love is patient. It knows when to act. Judah knew this and waited for the right moment to plead with his father.

So we now see a matured Judah able to respectfully reason with their father over the releasing of Benjamin to them. This conversation is night and day in respect to Reuben and Jacob's. Here are some of the differences that qualify Judah to receive the title leader over his brothers:

a. Unlike Reuben, Judah pleads with his father to put the fault on him if Benjamin doesn't return. He didn't offer his future (his children) as a ransom but offered his own life. Sound familiar? Jesus laid down for us so we can have salvation today.

113

b. *Colossian 4:6 ~ Let your speech always be with grace, seasoned with salt, that ye may know how you ought to answer every man.* A leader that belittles and talks down to people is an inadequate one. Your tongue carries life and death: like Judah season your speech with grace to obtain favor with man.

c. Praise is a strategic weapon. It knows how to strike and when. Reuben's timing to speak to his father was a grave oversight. But Judah who waited on the leading of the Lord knew exactly when to reason with his father. Praise will accomplish what other things can't. Live a praise-filled life. In that place God reveals strategy and answers to road blocks you can't get past.

d. Judah is requesting the release of Benjamin not for a personal need but for the sake of survival for Jacob's household. A mature praiser honors leadership and looks out for the well-being of others by requesting the impossible for their benefit. A mature praiser is a prophetic intercessor, who pleads to God on behalf of others, for their success, health and prosperity. But mainly pleads to God for others so that GOD is glorified. (As Moses pleaded to God for the sake of HIS name).

Judah's words are heard and Jacob permits Benjamin to travel with his other sons to Egypt. That's the power of praise. In due season it releases the impossible. Jacobs equips his sons with the best fruits in the land to purchase more corn; a little balm (healing), a little honey (health), spices (flavor), myrrh (humility), nuts and almonds and double the money to buy new corn and pay for the first round that was given for free. Praise releases heaven to fund the mission you are embarking. There is provision for the mission!

How powerful that Judah (praise) was able to take Benjamin (your victorious nature, your faith) with him to Egypt. I could write a whole separate book on the revelation flowing from that gesture, My God of Zion!!! Benjamin (your faith, will power and the power of your name) gave those men access to a place they had never been to before: Joseph's house. The Benjamin in you will grant you access to places you could never enter before. Just like Esther (a daughter of the tribe of Benjamin) found favor in the sight of the king and he extended his scepter to grant her access into his presence, when all had been previously denied. When God makes your name great, He will use YOUR NAME BENJAMIN to open doors [to the house of the governor] that you had no access to earlier. Benjamin means son of my strength or son of my right hand. The right hand is seen to possess power, influence, and strength in many cultures. Benjamin carried with him the anointing of strength and power (the anointing of grace), that seizes an opportunity and wins. Benjamin hand in hand with Judah (who is also meekness) has a powerful quiet influence that always produces victory without saying a word. His presence alone speaks volumes, and was enough to release Simeon from prison. Reuben is the beginning of Jacob's strength and Benjamin is, as the last born, represents his new strength. Do now you see more of who you are on the inside? This is who you are!!!

The story continues with Joseph testing his brothers by framing Benjamin as having stolen his golden goblet, with the punishment that the 10 were to go free and Benjamin would remain as a slave to Joseph. Again Judah (not Reuben) protests and pleaded for Joseph to keep them all. Joseph would not accept and demanded Benjamin be enslaved. But Judah proceeded to speak with Joseph as the mature leader he had become; showing us yet again how powerful praise is:

e. Gen. 44v18: *"Then Judah came near unto him."*

God is everywhere and always near us, but in worship we can dwell and abide in that intimate secret place with Christ. Praise and especially worship is like laying our head on the chest of God and listening to his heartbeat. It is intimate, personal and beautiful. Judah stepped away from his feelings (Reuben), his flesh (Simeon imprisoned), his judgement (Dan), his finances (Zebulun), his health (Asher), etc., and to speak privately with destiny; just him and Joseph. When all else around you looks hopeless, look into your spirit that lives the God to knows how to communicate with your promise. Your spirit is in touch with God's promise over your life. Listen to it and not your mind, your flesh, your body or your surroundings (the guards coming to take Benjamin away). Like Elijah, his spirit heard the promise which was the abundance of rain and refused to accept any evidence that didn't line up with that. In this place of worship, the Spirit of God uploads his word in to your spirit, which then downloads the message to the rest of you.

f. Judah acknowledged who Joseph was and honored his leadership and power. By showing him, this level of respect is the spirit of excellence at work. One's conviction on a matter does not permit them to be rude to others, especially those in leadership (Daniel 1). Our decorum is a tool God uses to receive favor with man.

Also remember that no matter the circumstance, speaking to God from a place of praise aligns your soul and body to receive from God. It's not flattery or manipulation but rather that acknowledging the power of God creates an atmosphere for revelation to flow. Just like Peter, his revelation of who Jesus was, allowed him to find out his purpose (a rock on which the church would be built).

g. Praise remembers and presents its case (44v19-31)
    · What has God said; stand on that, decree it, praise Him for it and bless Him for it; praise Him
    · Knows the will of God and declares "Lord you said."
    · It doesn't whine nor complain but speaks with confidence and articulation.
    · He moved in forgiveness and laid aside the years of neglect he felt by his father and spoke life for the sake of the days ahead. Praise speaks from a place of new beginnings.

h. Gen. 43v9 and Gen. 44v32-33; Praise or the life that praises God gives of itself and is selfless. Judah asked for the blame to be on his head if something went wrong with Benjamin, to his father first, then to Joseph when Benjamin is to be enslaved. He took on the blame as he promised his father. Isn't that what Jesus did for us? It sure is! He put aside his innocence, majesty and comfort to save us from the death we deserved and hell and in exchange for us to live in eternity with Him in glory. The spirit man esteems others higher than itself and a life of praise exists to set others free.

i. Gen. 45v1; Joseph reveals himself when Judah speaks. At the right time, the right place and the right moment, praise will unlock what is hidden. Keep praising God during those times when you don't know what to do and when you are backed up in a corner as Judah and his brothers were. Praise and worship God in all that you do and that which is hidden will be revealed.

Chapter 13
My Journal Entry

(This is an excerpt from my journal in 2010, as I studied on the life of Joseph)

The reality of Joseph's life is very tough when you are living it daily. It's so easy to read it because you see the beginning to the end from a reader's point of view. It has a very happy ending. But now I find that it's a whole different ball game living it daily, especially when you are in the pit, in some form of slavery, falsely accused or in the dungeon for choosing holiness. The reality of it is not always the easiest pill to swallow. Day by day, as I stay in God's word I find myself content in this place because I am where the Lord wants me to be. I am learning to be content. Learning equals practice, homework, listening, paying close attention, working on projects, participation, testing, and passing, failing and applying. I wonder how many nights Joseph cried himself to sleep and how many moments he had to brush off frustration and fatigue and refuse to give up.

He pressed passed the desire to give up or be bitter, despite not having any rights as a slave. I wonder how many times he gave himself a pep talk to keep going when the going got tough and when it seemed that all the odds were against him. Reminding himself that he was special, called and ordained, and how often did he recite the dreams God gave him? Did he remind himself of the words spoken over him by his father in those moments he spent mentoring him? Was he holding onto the promise so that he would hope knowing the dungeon was not his destination? I know one thing is certain, it was not easy, but Joseph's attitude was exemplary. He was just as human as I am, with hopes and dreams, goals and desires, etc.

One thing about Joseph that I love is his example to press through the uncertainty and how faithful he was even though his surroundings gave him the right to be bitter, detached, and mediocre. He couldn't get himself out of his situation, even if he tried. His request to be remembered by the butler when he got out was "forgotten" and only God orchestrated his release from jail. Only God can remove me from this situation. There are lessons that the Lord is teaching me that I must learn. Surely it cannot all be for nothing… It hurts to be here sometimes; hurt to be overlooked over and over. Hurt to be rejected and betrayed. And even some moments it hurts to wait; but I am learning that my attitude must change. My attitude determines the posture of my mind which determines my humility. My mind bows down, Lord! One thing is for sure: I desperately want to please God each day and be faithful to Him. I don't know how to give up on Him because he is my life. He is my strength and my world. Giving up on Him is giving up on life and on my purpose. He has the words to life and so leaving Him is not an option. HE IS MY LIFE!

I am learning to be content and praise God as I wait. All this revelation is powerful and applicable. So how can I fail? How can I fail if God is for me? I will have a great attitude about this because He is shaping and molding me. I will serve Him with excellence in the dungeon, excellence in the pit and excellence in the waiting place. I will serve Him with joy because He is a faithful God who truly deserves my worship, whether I'm in the best of situations or not. Joseph learned from his father that God deserved the glory no matter what the circumstances looked like or no matter how contrary life went to the promise. Will God only be praised when all is well? Will He only be praised when I'm happy and on the mountain tops? He must be praised then and always! My life belongs to Him in the good and the bad. He will be worshipped! He will be praised because I love Him and He loves me! He is GOD!

I'm embracing that being chosen doesn't always mean smooth sailing. I have known this, but must now become one with it. It involves tears, joys, laughter, endurance, stretching, and ups and downs. Job said to his wife, "Shall we receive good only at the hand of God and not receive evil?" In all, I'm leaning the sovereignty of God and learning to worship Him in all circumstances.

I'm learning to fight the battles on my knees in prayer rather than talking about them. Naphtali was blessed to speak good words. The Naphtali in me is being trained to speak good words even when I don't feel like it, even when the situation calls for insults, extreme anger and disappointment. May the spirit of Naphtali rise and shine in me and may my speech be pleasing to the Lord and bring life to all that hear it. After all, what use is a promise if my tongue will kill it with vicious words!

Another hard pill to swallow daily is when there is nothing I can do to get out of this situation. There is no offering, no tithe, no equation, scheme, plan, process, principle etc. that can be implemented to get out of the dungeon. This is my classroom. The place God has decided to save me from my [limited] will and mold me into his marvelous design. He creates masterpieces in the oddest of places, and here I am. Being developed in the darkness of the dungeon (sigh), the uncomfortable, so-not-me dungeon; and all the while my response is and must be, "thank you Lord for choosing me." Thank you for seeing me fit by your grace to handle this assignment. Protect my heart from failing; protect my eyes from what they will see in here and give me your perspective. I need a divine exchange in here. My weakness for your strength, my sorrow for your joy, and my mediocrity for your excellence. In here I am experiencing an awakening, like being re-born, and upgraded. I like this new Me operating in confidence, strength, kindness, fearlessness, etc. at levels I never thought I'd attain this quickly.

The only way to come out of here is when You, Lord, say I am ready and matured for the destiny ahead. My character must sustain me at the altitudes I'm soaring to. Character that is ready to stand before "my Pharaoh!" As long as Pharaoh never had those dreams, Joseph stayed in the dungeon. Lord my prayer, then, is make me ready to be a problem-solver and not a spectator or participator in the chatter of what is wrong. Make me a solution to crises both big and small, to kings and leaders, children and widows, to people from all walks of life. Use my "ME" to be the Jesus some will see. So that you will one day say "well done my good and faithful servant, you were my hands and feet." I know I ask a hard thing but this dungeon has made me dream for the impossible. Help me be sensitive to the leading of Holy Spirit that I will be ready to aid others. I understand that not every battle will be my assignment so Father, expose the crisis you desire me to fix. In the meantime, please sharpen my ear to hear interpretations and revelations from your heart and mind. Give me clarity and boldness of speech to speak your truth to any man I stand before. I can't do this without you Lord. I'm desperate for your glory to rest on my life. Desperate for the new sound you are about to release in me. Help me, Lord and fall fresh on me. Prepare me to stand before Pharaoh. Prepare to stand before every opportunity you have in store for me. Never underestimating the power of a divine encounter!

Friend, if you don't journal talk with God, I encourage you to. Let Him know how you feel about your experiences. He is not so untouched by our infirmities that He won't understand. Jesus coming to earth was so powerful because we have an eternal reminder that Christ knows how we feel. He knows how it feels to be hungry, angry, disappointed, betrayed, lied about and alone. He truly understands the struggles we face as people. He lived without sin yet knows our struggles and He provided victory through the cross for these storms of life. Throughout scripture we see that those who lived as open books before God had success through the trials; they were transparent with God, even in their mess, fear, frailty and cowardice. Their short comings did not disqualify them to be used greatly by God: Abraham, Isaac, Jacob, Asaph (Ps. 73), David (Bathsheba, Solomon, Ps 51), Elijah (1 kings 19), Jeremiah (Jer. 20), Gideon (Judges 6), Peter.

You are not disqualified because of what you do not possess but rather the perfect candidate for the miraculous with the little you do have. God has chosen and called you for such a time as this to do exploits. In boldness, enter your destiny and possess what God has for you. Don't stop dreaming and hoping and looking ahead. Don't let your dream die! No matter how hopeless it seems, know that God is in control and has already made a way out of this. Pray for mind renewal and an attitude adjustment that you may flow in the spirit of excellence right where you are. Failing a test with God only means you have to stay where you are and re-take it. His desire is to always advance us but just like a good parent doesn't give their child access to luxuries and responsibilities they are not ready for, so our Heavenly Father does the same. He will not jeopardize your well-being by ill-equipping you for LIFE .So praise him in your dungeon, embrace the shine it's polishing on you. Praise him like Paul and Silas did at the midnight hour that an earthquake broke their chains. They were broken to show them and us, through revelation, that our circumstances have no hold on us. We are free because of Christ in us. That's why He went to Calvary to set us free from bondage, even captivity of the pit and dungeon you are in today. He opened up our eyes to give us hope and a future.

Chapter 14
The Reality of Destiny

Sometimes we think and fall into the trap that once we're in destiny, all will be perfect. The grass is greener on the other side mentality. It is greener, but there's so much needed to keep it that green. Many get there and find the bed of roses has thorns or issues that they least expected to find. There is a whole new reality as to who true friends are, haters and critics are coming out of the woodwork, (potential) lawsuits follow, pressure beyond their imagination arise every hour and expectations don't go away. As the Lord takes his people, from glory to glory, there will be opposition at each level. Paul, in 2 Corinthians 12, stated that even at the height of spiritual maturity and greatness he had reached, or the magnitude of the revelations (the logos, third heaven and paradise experiences) he'd experienced, he could not pray away the thorn in his flesh, the messenger of Satan sent to torment him (but benefitted Paul in keeping him humble).

Joseph is now one of the most powerful men in the world. The world is about to face a famine and he has the divinely inspired solution. He is clothed in wealth and adorned with power (Pharaoh's signet ring) and rides in leadership (second chariot to Pharaoh; all those who saw him in his chariot paid obeisance to him). He is the envy of anyone desiring power, respect, status, authority and prestige. At age 30, he is an accomplished young man who has it all: a new job, a wife, power, recognition, wealth, restoration, retribution, respect, a title, servants, a mansion, new friends, the new life, the status of leadership he saw in his dreams (especially the second one) and the greatness he sensed in his spirit. He had arrived, almost surreal but his dream had manifested. The dream which was once so distant had now become a reality, OVERNIGHT.

In the last chapters of Genesis, we are privileged to get a glimpse of Joseph's life in destiny and after the promotion. In most stories, not just fairytales, there is a huge dramatic ending of happily-ever-afters and greener pastures of comfort and ease. An illusion is created that few problems of no great magnitude exist, and money solves all problems. We are in for a rude awakening! Anyone living in increase, if they are honest, will tell you that the bed of roses has thorny moments. Joseph still had to deal with a few thorns.

Accepted Leadership?

Joseph is clearly, without question, and undeniably chosen as an adequate leader and governor over Egypt. His promotion is noised throughout all Egypt and is very well known. This Hebrew slave and convict was promoted to governor. This was a very coveted position by many dignitaries. If this position never existed, it does now because of Joseph. There is no other reason that he is here. (Prophetic nugget: May God create positions just for you)! Why then, in 41v54-55, do the people when the famine comes, refuse to follow protocol and go to Pharaoh instead of Joseph? In the seventh Year, they gave a portion of their harvest to Joseph, who was overseer of the project. I believe that there is a time and place to go to the top in the chain of command, but not in every circumstance. It is imperative to respect the chain of command put in place so that the main or head leader doesn't have burnout or produce low quality results because he or she is not gifted in that area. A good leader delegates so they can focus their resources on other matters that desperately need their attention. Pharaoh had to send them to Joseph when they cried to him for the soreness of the famine. Publically, they celebrate you and secretly, they don't look up to you as the leader you are. Money doesn't change everything. JUST REMEMBER THAT. May we be as Paul, who learned to be content in all situations, whether much or little. Choose to enjoy and love life no matter what season.

Traditional Mindsets

There are certain battles that will only be done away with, with Christ's return. The grave injustices and hardships we have faced for centuries have either diminished because of man's fight for independence and equality or waxed in wickedness as men become lovers of themselves. That doesn't mean that we stop fighting for justice, but rather recognize that by Christ's return, and the creation of a new heaven and earth, will sin be completely eradicated. Your promotion will not fix every injustice nor be spared from it. In Gen. 43v32; we are introduced to an Egyptian custom that forbids them to eat meals with Hebrews because it was an abomination. According to historians, Egyptians worshipped all types of gods, even cows, so they were seen as sacred. Hebrew Shepherds were therefore an abomination because they ate cows. They felt the same way with other cultures, not just the Hebrews. Although Pharaoh did give them Goshen, the best of the land, and to tend his own herds, it was an abomination to eat with them. Therefore Joseph had to live with this knowledge and live with them in peace. You've got to have some tough skin to deal with things like that.

Dysfunctional Family (His Paternal Family)
The most powerful man in the world has a horrible secret and past. His own brothers, who share his last name, father and are his blood, hate him with a vengeance. The fact that he is alive was God showing favor through Judah. They plotted to kill him for his giftedness from God, nothing that he himself, Joseph fabricated. This glorious time in his life would be perfect if those closest to him were around or in his life, but they weren't. They missed out on his crowning moment. God so transformed his life that when they did see him, they didn't even recognize him. Even after his promotion, for seven years, he doesn't go home. Was he held at peace by the Lord or did he think going back would cause problems for his brothers? Had he accepted himself as not being part of them? Why didn't he go back to see if his father was still alive? Was he afraid to find his father dead and left at the open untamed cruelty of his brothers? He has children that have not met his people and hear these horrific tales of them (except about Jacob). There is no interaction from his father's household. Even in this case, we are reminded that money, elevation and status don't solve everything.

Vulnerability and Transparency
Joseph cried bitterly when he saw his brothers and remembered his dreams as they bowed before him. He cried secretly every time he saw them and when he saw Benjamin. When he revealed himself to them, he wept openly to them. As stated earlier, his weeping was heard in Pharaoh's house, too, among the servants. This powerful governor, with the power (signet ring) of Pharaoh, cried openly as he reconciled with his brothers. The deep love he had for them is transparent and Christ-like that he immediately lets them into his inner circle as friends. You've

got to know who your 'inner circle family' is to you. It must be divinely discerned because not everyone can handle the real you and love you as you are (transparency). Some people keep their enemies close as" frenemies" so they can keep a close eye on them. You don't have to. Not everyone who is smiling in your face, tending to your beck and call and faithfully serving you, should be in your inner circle. Use the wisdom and discernment of God to determine your level of friendship with people. Jesus had many friends. He had thousands, then 120, then 70, then the disciples and the women, then the 12, then the 3, then 1 (John).

Crisis within the Crisis

No matter how well you plan, there are unforeseen crises and problems that will occur and need your immediate attention. Destiny will demand more of you. Are you ready? To whom much is given, much is required (Luke 12:48). Mid chapter 47, the money to buy the stored food ran out for the Egyptians. And Joseph's execution of the matter shows the need for continued operations in excellence in destiny. Be forever thinking, planning, and advancing, to avoid stagnant and irrelevance. So much depended on Joseph: from running a kingdom to investing in the survival of Egyptians and many others across the earth. He had to seek the Lord on how to provide for them without exploiting them for his personal gain. Even then, we see money doesn't answer everything. Money and destiny did not prevent the soreness of the famine. They could only prepare for it.

Questions:

He meets his brother for the first time. Either when he was sold Benjamin wasn't born or was very young as a baby. It's an emotional time for him. It's like discovering a whole new piece of yourself that you have to learn all over again. What was Benjamin like? Would he and Joseph get along? What would life be like if they'd grown up together? Did his father ever think of him or try to look for him? Was Benjamin to suffer the same fate as he did at the hands of their half - brothers? He had to find out who they were and who they had become over the years. On the flip side, his older brothers question their brother's loyalty to them, especially after their father Jacob dies. Joseph puts their fears to rest and assures them, but this is 17 years later that they reveal their feelings (Gen. 47v28 and Gen. 50v15). This is a family with a lot questions. I wonder what Jacob said when he found out what his oldest ten sons did to Joseph. Did he understand because of what Esau and Laban had put him through? Yes, every family has issues, questions and situations that need worked out or are working on that money, prestige, and promotion cannot fix.

Hidden, sharpened, and polished as an arrow in Jacob's quiver Joseph learns the importance of keeping an arrow-filled quiver of his own for excellent leadership.

a. Arrow One: have a voice that speaks [voices that speak] truth into your life; in chapter 48, Jacob continues to be that voice that speaks life over and wisdom into his children. Even when Joseph doesn't agree with him about the birthright blessings of his sons Ephraim and Manasseh (it displeased him actually [Gen 48v17]), but he was able to humble himself to his father's wisdom and discernment. Despite his status as most powerful man in the earth, Joseph submitted himself to the counsel of a voice that spoke the truth in love to correct him. I think that Joseph is trying to prevent the consequences of favoritism that he suffered with brothers amongst his sons. But the love of his father puts his mind at ease so that the baton is passed on. Do not despise the wisdom of the counselors (parents, mentors, leadership etc.) God places in your life to speak what you need to hear and not what you always want to hear.

b. Arrow Two: No matter how powerful we become at any level in life, let praise (Judah) always have influence in our lives. Never stop praising God and giving him glory; speaking to him from a place of worship and reverence. In the atmosphere of praise God speaks, moves, and counsels in tremendous ways. Judah was the only one able to convince and Joseph, the powerful governor, with his gentle words, concerning his cup found in Benjamin's sack of grain. It was at that moment that Joseph was no longer able to conceal his identity and revealed himself to his brothers. Judah goes hand in hand with humility. In order to worship God, your mind and heart must bow to him with honor, respect and humility. It is with humility and meekness that earth is inherited and power entrusted; just as we saw in Jesus. Humility is power. It is great strength under great control, a life that knows God is in control of everything. It is a life that loves God passionately in worship. Every level of elevation or promotion requires a more intense expression of praise and worship. The higher he'll take you, the deeper and lower your life [worship] must bow before him.

c. Arrow Three: Remember the purpose of this promotion (Gen. 50v20)

(Joseph, Esther and Daniel). It was not for the fancy clothes, the gold chain (worn by leaders and dignitaries) the chariot ridden after Pharaoh, the house, the prestige, or honorable marriage. Although those were wonderful gifts and accolades from God that Joseph received, the core purpose was to glorify God and to preserve the line of Abraham and honor their covenant (Gen. 45v11, 47v12, 50v20-21). Staying focused on why God has blessed us in a specific way of promotion, will keeps us humble and faithful to the vision. Like Esther, you are here for a specific purpose, here for a time such as this (Esther 4v14), not just to be gloriously decorated as royalty. You are here, [Esther] to be used by God to preserve His people. Your core purpose will always keep you from wasting resources because you have direction and strategy.

d. Arrow Four: Remember where God has brought you from (fore fathers). Gen. 48v15; How God kept those before you, he is faithful to keep you too. Their powerful testimonies encouraged Joseph in the pit, in the dungeon, and in the palace. Heb. 12v1 says there is a cloud of witnesses surrounding, supporting, and cheering us on that have run this race, as well. They have passed the baton to us and are cheering for us to run well to the end. We can always look to the God for instruction and direction on all things pertaining to life and Godliness; nothing is new under the sun. Remember those that sacrificed with you, invested in you and believed in you when no one knew your name. Success will require much of you, but take time to honor those that honored you in the pit. But also take the time to forgive, bless and pray for those that hurt you along the way. Their resentment and rejection was used to take you to incredible and influential platforms. They made you stronger for the journey and loving them is the evidence of genuine love as Jesus stated.

e. Arrow Five: *"Chapter 10: Godly Character."* Remember your life is a light. Others are watching your every move. Whether they despise or adore you, your testimony will speak volumes to them [especially when you live a life that glorifies God]. The overnight transition from convict to governor would require rapid adjustments to how Joseph lived his private life. The order of the prison is more casual than the protocol of the palace. Although the principles are similar, the expectations are not. Daniel and his friends had to be taught for three years in science, knowledge and protocol in order to serve in the palace. Your life will speak to many:

make the spirit of excellence (love, etiquette, demeanor, and quality) your best friend in order to shine and excel in the palace.

f. Arrow Six: Live in the shadow of the Almighty. The shadow represents many dimensions of God, but for this arrow I want to focus on the facet of his sovereignty. That his will must always prevail, with our thoughts being his thoughts, and our perspective being his perspective, and our ways being his ways. Genesis 50v15-21: (Emphasis on verse 19) "and Joseph said unto them, Fear not; for am I in the place of God?" Joseph's brothers are fearful for their lives now that Jacob has died and assume Joseph will seize the moment to release his wrath on them. But Joseph, a man of integrity and impeccable character has a life surrendered to leadership and sovereignty of God. The answer to his brothers was powerful and showed the compassionate heart Joseph. He had forgiven his brothers because he feared God. Just like he feared God and would not sin against him by sleeping with Potiphar's wife, he feared God in how he treated his brothers. Use your promotion as a platform to bless and not curse; to forgive and empower, to nourish and sustain, to honor and show love. Leaving vengeance to God is honoring his Lordship and sovereignty. The men they had become were different from the men they were decades prior. Be the leader that sees the bigger picture remembering that some people will hurt you from place of their shortcomings (insecurities, hurts, and immaturity).

Refuse to be the leader that defiles their platform with selfish ambitions, looking down on others, seizing opportunities to exercise revenge, and developing a god- like complex. Remember the assignment. You are a vessel for change in the earth. A conduit for God to manifest his will in the earth. In the classroom of Potiphar's house Joseph learned God always had the only and final on matters of the heart. He did not live as the final word in his life, but it was always the word of God that prevailed. The wisdom in Deuteronomy 8 still stands today that we are not to exercise our power and authority to fulfill the lusts of the flesh, but rather remember that we are still servants to serve those we lead. Paul, as an example, described himself a servant and slave of Jesus Christ destined to serve God's people. Be the servant leader that makes a difference in the earth.

Chapter 15
Strip your Reuben of power

Gen. 49v3-4: *"Reuben thou art my firstborn, my might, and the beginning of my strength, the excellency of dignity, and the excellency of power; Unstable as water, thou shalt not excel, because thou went up to thy father's bed, then defiled thou it: he went up to thy couch."*

It is very important that we understand how powerful Reuben was and the influence he had or should have had on his brothers. We need to look at why his father blessed him this way and why, according to scripture, he was stripped of his birthright (double portion) and title as chief ruler of his family.

1 Chronicles 5v1-2: *"Now the sons Reuben the first born of Israel. For he was the first born; but for as much as he defiled his father's bed, his birthright was given unto the sons of Joseph the son of Israel; and the genealogy is not reckoned after the birthright. For Judah prevailed above his brethren and of him came the chief ruler; but the birthright was Joseph's."*

Reuben represents our soul, our feelings, emotions and intellect; and even the mind. Jacob described him as the mighty beginning of his strength, excellence of dignity and power, but yet unstable. Our feelings, emotions and minds are very powerful parts of us and play extremely influential roles in our lives. We make major and minor everyday decisions from this place. It's a very important part of us that must be in great condition for how much we function from it. Our Reuben being stripped of its birthright, is no small matter to ignore or take lightly and this chapter explains why.

We form opinions on things very quickly based on our intellect, emotions, and feelings. As first born, our Reuben almost always has the first say so on a matter. Feelings are not bad and we should never desire to not feel. The ability to cry, happiness, anger and frustration are blessings that distinguish humans from creation:

- Crying and rejoicing with others is important (Romans 12v15)
- Laughter is medicine (Proverbs 17v22)
- Be angry but sin not (Ephesians 4v26)
- Timidity will show up but refuse to live there (Judges 6)
- Frustrated but remained in holiness (Jeremiah 20)

Reuben houses your intellect, logic, common sense, and ability to reason. This is the part of you that is strongly influenced by experience, education, and environment. The soul is powerful and extremely important. It is the beginning of our strength indeed, with the ability to influence every part of our being. But its instability (emotions, feelings, intellect ever changing) makes it an unsuitable (main/chief) leader. It must fall subject to the will of God. Jacob told Reuben he shall not excel, meaning his strength would only so accomplish to a limited capacity concerning certain things. A good education is important but will only take you so far. Supernatural is supernatural and can only be lived out or experienced when the spirit man (Judah) gets involved as the lead. (Education is an important asset, but must never replace nor be synonymously used with God's wisdom).

Hebrews 4v12 says that God's word clearly divides the soul and the spirit (notice it doesn't say the spirit and the flesh). The Holy Spirit uses the Word of God to de-robe our soul of its chief leadership role and gives it to the spirit man, as did Jacob to Reuben and Judah. When we die to self or pick up our cross daily (Jacob on his death bed) then are we (Jacob) able to speak the proper positioning of the Israel within us. Only when the sun (Jacob) goes down, are the stars (Israel/his sons) able to shine. Judah must lead your life, for it is he who lives in spiritual places, is perfected and communes with God. The spirit will cause permanent change whilst the soul (Reuben) specializes in temporary fixes. When we worship God in spirit and truth (John 4) we worship him from a place that guarantees change. And God's word will rightly divide a soul-*ish* worship experience from the Spirit led one. We are to worship God with our whole being which includes our feelings and emotions; but they must not be the lead in worship but rather worship in response to what is happening in our spirit (Judah). If the soul leads in worship, the temporary fix will not withstand the attacks on Monday or that month and leave an individual discouraged and bound. Worship God in spirit and truth and be changed forever.

Genesis 37:29 – And Reuben returned unto the pit, and behold, Joseph was not in the pit and rent his clothes (ripped his clothes in sorrow). And he returned unto his brothers, and said, 'the child is not; and I where shall I go?'

Reuben in this story did not fully understand and embrace his position of power. In earlier verses he hears his brothers plotting to kill Joseph and saves him by suggesting they throw him in a pit. Then he disappears (delegates responsibility) and returns later to find a mess (because he didn't regulate the process). A good leader regulates (checks in, monitors, adjusts, DOES NOT MICRO-MANAGE) what they have delegated so they can duplicate themselves effectively. Reuben is a reactionary type leader with no long-term vision planning skills (Gen. 37v29-30 and Gen. 42v22). He willingly offers two of his sons to be killed to make a vow with his father when he denies Egypt's request to have Benjamin leave (Gen. 42v36-38). The same two sons of four that would carry his name in 1 Chronicles 5! No generational planning. Your Reuben will sacrifice today what will sustain you tomorrow. Men of greatness are separated from average men because they take authority and do what is right, no matter the cost. Reuben had the excellence of power and dignity, but refused to use it to do extraordinary things. Your intellect will come up with amazing things, but will never yield the results birthed from your spirit man (Judah). Let your Reuben work in submission to your spirit man and see how much brighter your emotions, feelings, and intellect will shine!

Your Reuben has no real authority over the flesh (Simeon) and is often conflicted between listening to your Simeon or Judah or itself (doing what feels right vs what is holy vs what makes sense). It knows (and loves) God from a place of knowledge and feelings. It can actually mature in knowledge and appear wise, but remain dwarf- like in the Spirit. We must be very careful as leaders in the body of Christ to not be Reuben type leaders but rather die to self so the Jacob in us can properly appoint his twelve to shine. If we are to make a major difference in the earth the Reuben/soulish Christian must surrender his/her current nature and allow the Joseph anointing to begin the transformation in them to become Israel. Or else we will continue to see Rueben at work causing chaos in the body. Especially leaders, ordained minsters, etc. beware of Reuben -like tendencies:

a. First with boundaries and crossing them: Reuben slept with his father's concubine. Your platform is not to be used to say what you want, do what you want, feel as you want. It is given by God complete with boundaries and guidelines to be used for his glory to empower others and set order. But Reuben flirts with boundary lines because he has not grasped that intellect and logic must surrender to and not fight against the will of God.

b. They are leaders who have the power to make a difference, but don't because of negligence. He knows what Simeon and Levi are capable of and hears all his brothers (except Benjamin) plot to kill Joseph, but Reuben steps away to take care of his personal endeavors. He leaves his vision (Joseph) in the hands of irresponsible people. You will give an account of what you did with the Josephs God placed in your care Reuben. Treat them well and allow them to bloom.

c. A Reuben leader takes responsibility over an issue, with one goal in mind to protect and promote SELF. There is zero to little regard of how positive or negative actions will affect others. Because with Reuben it's all about ME. Note the difference with Judah even in his immature state pleads with his brothers to not kill Joseph lest his blood be on THEIR hands, "for he is OUR brother and OUR flesh (Gen 37:26-27). Whereas Reuben says, "Oh, no what will happen to ME?" (Gen. 37v30).

d. They are leaders that do "enough good" during tough times. This is a perfect example of having a form of Godliness but lacking its power (2 Timothy 3:5). Saying the right things, doing the right things, but no inner deep rooted conviction of the outward proclamations. It is all a front because they are very secretly dysfunctional, unstable or insecure. Their motives are questionable, and actions confusing. Reuben cared for Joseph but not enough to send him back home away from his brothers' wrath. He wanted to punish Joseph because Reuben's well hidden insecurity of mediocrity was always exposed by Joseph's natural flowing excellence. Reubens are intimidated by Josephs because they are dreamers and visionaries and go to great lengths to silence them by manipulation of feelings, emotions and intellect. Reubens do dream as well but not to the capacity of Josephs. Josephs are radical, over the top dreamers and although they don't verbally challenge Reubens their lifestyles do. Joseph possessed what they would naturally love to have favor, prosperity, and impeccable character. Naturally, the first born should stand out, but when a Joseph is present, a Reuben leader will feel threatened. A perfect example of this is King Saul (a Reuben leader) who was intimidated by David (a Judah/Joseph Leader).

This Reuben in us must be stripped of his title immediately and positioned to be renewed and prosper in God. Jesus did not give up on your soul and paid a heavy price to restore its purpose and influence in your life. It must not be ignored, but rather taught how to operate under the direction of the Holy Spirit, who is the Spirit of love, power, and a sound mind. Out of all Joseph's brothers, Reuben saw injustice and favoritism in his household even before Joseph was born. He saw Jacob love Rachel more than his own mother Leah was loved. He saw Rachel's desperation to have children and desiring his fertility plants which he had obtained. God had closed her womb when he saw that Leah was being despised and Rachel favored and loved. As you have grown from infancy to adulthood, experience has come to be a close friend. Your Reuben has seen a lot and cannot be trusted to be the lead any more. Strip it of its birthright and live by the Spirit.

Are you willing to have your wavering feelings, emotions and intellect guide your flesh (Simeon), physical body (Levi), your spirit (Judah), intuition/instinct (Issachar), tongue (Naphtali), health (Asher), promise/dominion (Joseph), wisdom/judgment (Dan), finances (Zebulun), warrior (Gad) and willpower/faith (Benjamin)? When they stand alone each one is a crucial part of you that takes years and seasons to develop and mature. Each one requires the expert care and nurturing love of the Holy Spirit and the Lordship of Jesus Christ to form a mature spiritual Israel. Let your Judah reign in your life. When made alive in God by salvation it stays in constant communication with him, downloading to your mind revelation from God. It openly receives divine thoughts from its source in whose image and likeness it was created.

The importance in stripping Reuben is based on a major principle found in kingdom leadership. Amendments are made to laws in democracies but not in kingdoms because a king or queen's word once written as a law is final. If they changed laws it was a sign of weakness and being feeble minded. Their word was their bond and a symbol of authority. That's why the centurion told Jesus "just send your word." When Adam sinned, the law of sin and death came into existence in the earth. Because God the Father is THE KING OF KINGS, he made a new law, the Law of the Spirit and of Life through Jesus Christ. The first Adam operated in Reuben leadership and the second Adam in Judah/Joseph leadership. If the old Adam (Reuben) was replaced with the new Adam/Jesus (Judah), the same change must happen in you before you forfeit your Eden.

Chapter 16
Living an abundant Life

Personally, so much, has come alive to me as I have been writing this book. Each chapter I wrote was from a place of the Holy Spirit having worked or working in that area in my life. So none of this is theory to me; I have seen Jesus throughout these chapters and how like Judah, He put his life on the line to pay the debt for His brothers, and how like Joseph, He went ahead of his family to prepare a way for them. I can't end this book without referring to Jesus and who He is and what He has done for us.

Jesus is the only begotten son of Yahweh, God the Father. He is God the Son of the Godhead trinity. He is Alpha and Omega, the Beginning and the End. He is wonderful counselor, the Great I am, the Living Word, the Way, the Truth, and the Life. He is the eternal, most wise God. He is Salvation, Prince of peace, King of Kings and Lord of Lords. He is the Bread of Life, the Good Shephard, the Living Word, Immanuel, the Mighty God, and the Cloud by day and Pillar of fire by night. HE IS GOD.

This amazing God paid a great price for us on the Cross, a price we could never repay and we should never take lightly because it gives us eternal life. No amount of wealth combined from our beginning of time till the end would ever pay or match what Jesus did. We are forever grateful for His loving sacrifice, a sacrifice that changed the course of this world forever. John 3v16 says *"For God so loved this world that He gave his only begotten Son, that whosoever believes in Him should not perish but have everlasting life."* Never forgetting the power of the Cross, Christ also did this to help us experience life to its fullest.

Abundant life: John 10v10; "*I am come that they might have life, and that they might have it more abundantly.*" Jesus did a powerful work on the Cross. He called disciples, taught and trained them and sent them into the world making it possible for all of us to hear the gospel and have eternal life. Jesus came to give us back our Joseph experience which is to be fruitful, multiply, replenish, subdue and have true dominion. Never forgetting how important and powerful salvation is, Christ also died to give us an abundant life.

Hebrews 6v1-2, points this out very clearly, that we should get beyond only being saved. We need to have an understanding that we are saved for a purpose, to have relationship with God; and to shine forth the Kingdom of God here on earth with love, power and a sound mind, in the guidance, potential, anointing and direction of the Holy Spirit. Our choice of living any less is an insult to Jesus Christ and His mission here on earth. Believers have been put on this earth to do above and beyond. Settling, mediocrity, complacency, status quo and consequence are words that should not be manifested in the life of a believer. We have been called to excel, to soar and to have dominion. He raised the bar from the standard of the law to show us that, in Him, mediocrity is no longer an option.

Jesus taught and raised the bar:

- Every day is holy, not just the Sabbath
- Love your enemies and bless them too
- Sin happens in your heart (God judges our thoughts)
- The gospel is for all Jews and Gentiles, slave and free and male and female.
- The law of grace, in exchange of the law
- Life in the Holy Spirit
- Signs and wonders

Jesus raises the bar in these areas of our personal 12 within. In our Israel, mediocrity is no longer the only option:

- Reuben: Our souls must be renewed and subject to the Holy Spirit
- Simeon: The flesh must be imprisoned and executed daily
- Levi: Our physical bodies must be offered as living sacrifices (Romans 12v1)
- Judah: Our spirit, worship and praise rebirthed and made new (John 3)
- Zebulun: Finances used to glorify God and not to be a god

- Issachar: Instinct ever ready for the times and seasons
- Dan: Living in the wisdom of the Holy Spirit (Proverbs 8)
- Asher: To prosper in health even as our soul prospers
- Naphtali: Our speech controlled by the Holy Spirit (James 3)
- Gad: Being more than a conqueror for greater is He in us
- Joseph: Promise and destiny (dreams and visions)
- Benjamin: Your will power and the power of your name

Why do we accept average? Why have we concluded that more than enough is not an option? And I'm not talking about money? For some it might be, but let's look at the bigger picture of prosperity as was mentioned earlier in Chapter 6. Prosperity being that the Lord is evidently on our lives and we excel as the best janitors, moms, teaches, fathers, CEO's, entrepreneurs, construction workers, waiters, flight attendants, friends, family, employees, ministers, pastors, etc. We are called to bloom wherever we are planted and to passionately pursue the dream, vision and promise fashioned in your DNA.

There are many things stopping those in Christ from doing what they have been called to do: abuse, fear, insecurities, lack of identity, fatigue, hurt, no mentorship, location, ignorance, religion, sickness, finances, excuses and strongholds. God is great enough to bring forth all that is within you. He came to set us free from abuse and its scars, free from fear, insecurities, fatigue, hurt, etc. and set us on our way. He is able to fill us with His wisdom (of which we are strongly encouraged in James to just ask). He doesn't need our finances, neither is He limited by our disabilities, nor sickness to use our lives for His glory.

He is looking for us this hour to submit ourselves fully from our spirit man, the man made in His image, not the soulish man who is unstable. Jesus is amazing because He understands humanity and perfected it. He lived perfectly. He knows what it's like to be human and face its realities, frustrations, limitations, temptations and came and conquered, so we could live victoriously.

What is in your hand?

Sometimes we look so far outside of us for the answer, but Jesus has this brilliance of taking what is already in us and making it blossom for His glory. As you are reading this chapter and have read this book, I want to challenge you with some questions that (if you haven't already been asked) are extremely important.

1. What is your life's mission statement?
2. What did you dream of as a child?
3. What is in your hand?

These were the questions I had to answer as well. Deep inside of me were gifts that had already been placed for good works. I rested in submission and surrender, and I saw how they were mighty through God. No matter how small or little, each gift was great in the Master's hands. Listen, Jacob was good at cooking and it won him a birthright. Joseph was a dream interpreter and it took him before Pharaoh. Don't despise those things that come naturally to you. David's natural ability to kill the lion and the bear, prepared him to kill Goliath, intimidation-free. As I mentioned earlier, let God develop your gifts in secret that you might shine in public. It is in you and the methods God uses to bring them out though will not always be the easiest. Be encouraged that through it all Jesus understands and the Holy Spirit right there by your side. He is interceding to the Father on our behalf.

The word of God is a great place to start when looking for what is in your hands. The Lord always speaks to us from his word, ALWAYS. It is like a mirror, a lamp and a road map. I love the Rhema word (revelation) that comes from the Logos (written) word of God. Also the weekly assembly with other believers is another great way to find out what is in your hands. We are able, with the direction of the Holy Spirit, to speak into each other's lives:

- Tap into potential
- Give direction
- Call out and stir up gifts
- Prophesy
- Confirm and encourage gifts
- Sharpening of gifts
- Mentorship
- Discipleship

Jesus came to give us a rich (not monetary), full, joyful, life. PLEASE NOTE AGAIN, it doesn't mean all is perfect, but through the imperfections and struggles of life, we have a perfect Savior perfecting us. Jesus has a magnificent plan for your life. All he wants is your *"YES Lord, here is my life. I trust you with every fiber of my being that you are perfecting all that concerns me. Even those ugly, shameful things, you care about enough to transform me and save me from them."*

My prayer is that as we understand that as we know Christ, we will know more of ourselves and how He has awesomely equipped us to impact this world for the kingdom of God. Personally, both my hands are raised, because, frankly, not walking in my destiny is half living which feels like death.

Identity: Your identity is one of the major blessings in your hand, and Jesus came to restore it to you. His finished work on the cross undid the perversion caused by the fall of Adam. Our perception was tarnished in that fall and his opening up of blind eyes and setting captives free (Luke 4:18,19) has allowed the perception on our identity to take it's true form; that we are made in the image of God and are each an expression of the mind of God. He took how He would function and placed those thoughts, ideas and techniques into our spirits and new DNA. Not that we are God, but we are an expression of Him. What the enemy comes to do is to steal, kill and destroy (completely annihilate or to destroy as though it never existed) that identity and to pervert it so that our full potential is not reached, thus hurting the heart of God. The devil tempted Eve by offering her something she already had in God; his image and likeness. Satan doesn't know everything and we need to stop treating him like he does.

Listen to what the Holy Spirit says about that which he has already given you. Be encouraged that what is not naturally manifested, eternity is pregnant with for you. Ecclesiastes says that God hid eternity in our hearts therefore, faith is the sonogram of what eternity is pregnant with. That is your proof that your hopes are God-inspired. Faith is receiving what God has already said and declared and done in eternity, and in turn preparing for the due date on earth. It is not us telling God what we want Him to say or do. Faith is what we stand on, live by and speak from; therefore faith is speaking from one dimension into another. Speak what is (eternity) into the dimension of appearance (the natural). Hebrews 11v1 says "Now faith (God's word and promises are yes and amen) is the substance (the tangible proof from eternity) for the evidence of things not seen (of eternity spiritual matters not yet birthed in our time, to be realized as real by our physical natural senses). If we dwell in heavenly places (interact with the God head trinity, to listen, to tabernacle), we have access to certain truths and revelations that will help our lives here on earth. That is living out faith, (by faith and through faith).

Jesus and the help the Holy Spirit and God the Father are here aiding us, with understanding, love, grace, power and soundness of mind for us to be perfected and live out that abundant life Jesus died for. We also have cheerleaders who have run their races, cheering us on to do the same. *Hebrews 12v1-2; Wherefore seeing we also are compassed about with so great a cloud of witnesses, let us lay aside every weight, and the sin which so easily beset us, and let us run with patience the race that is set before us; looking unto Jesus the author and finisher of our faith: who for the joy that was set before him endured the cross, despising the shame, and is set down at the right hand of the throne of God."*

Hebrews 11 gives Biblical example of cheerleaders who have lived the abundant life Jesus offered us. What God did for them, he can and will do for us, too. There are various examples so that we can have at least one to relate to and learn what they did in their situation, to keep us encouraged and comforted that we win. Mine is Joseph, and the Lord allowed me to study his life and receive revelation and understanding for my benefit, my comfort, for strategy, for direction and shalom. The cloud of witnesses gone before me (including my heroes, my father and grandfather) has influenced my mental pathways to be paths of victory and success in Jesus. Their lives scream the greatness and power of God alive and strong in man. They are incredible examples of promise (faith + patience = promise) to me; anointed men of God called to do exploits and they did. We are blessed to be of a rich lineage form our father Abraham. May our children's children walk in greater heights and deeper depths!

Lay Aside the Weight

There are not sins, but rather situations, circumstances, mindsets, regrets, heartaches, ideologies, burdens, etc. that we have unnecessarily carried or allowed to stick to us along the way. As I watch my three little angels (Andrew, Cassandra and Eric) grow up I'm realizing that these babies' world of influence is expanding. My husband and I are still their greatest influence, but they are now in school, making friends and being exposed to more that will add positives and sadly introduce negatives (weights) into their lives. I'm not speaking ill on them but realizing that society plays a big role in shaping one's identity. A big role on teaching us how to pick up weights that we carry for years till they become they become second nature to us.

For some weights are:

- Walls we build to protect us from anticipated hurt, abandonment, neglect and mockery. It is not the healthy guarding of the heart the Bible encourages but rather guarded walls to not let people in because of living in fear. That is a weight keeping your from enjoying great relationship with people; Lay it aside!

- Mindsets are huge weights to carry; our way of thinking because of generational and society's influence. The way it has always been done. Grandma did it this way, so did dad and now, so will I. It's what we do. Being an innovative thinker takes guts to overcome the obstacles of being a pioneer. Therefore playing it safe is easier; Lay it aside!

- Burdens; The cares of this world that are real and some greater than others. They range from parents' sleepless nights concerned for their sick children or unsaved children, couples trying to put back pieces of hurt and broken marriages, mountainous unpaid bills, death of loved ones, injustices done to us, heartache covered from living in a broken world and ever increasing health issues. This is just to name a few examples of genuine concerns that weigh very heavily on the heart and mind, giving no answers for relief. They bring in discouragement and despair, making life unbearable. Then to add more fuel to the fire when bad doctrine is thrown in, these burdens cause implosions. Burdens and cares are not to be used synonymously with temptations (which are not more than we can bear). That verse has been taken out of context leaving many feeling like failures. Burdens are more than we can bear, and have a designated spot clearly stated in scripture; laid or cast down at the feet of Jesus. We can't fix them, change them and are not strong enough to carry them. God is strong enough to handle them unscathed. They don't cause Him depression, insomnia, frustration, weaknesses, sluggishness, worry or discontent. He handles them well because nothing is impossible with Him. Jesus' feet are here for you to lay down every burden, care or concern. Lay it down!

- Regrets: "I shoulda, coulda, woulda"; they are heavy on our minds, making one live in shame or denial of reality by reliving the glory days past their prime. The trap of failure starts to lure one in because the past, it seems, is where things were great. With having no power to undo time, this becomes a weight. Lost time is an impossible asset to replace. These need to be laid down in order to let your Israel function at its full capacity. Be free of this weight, the past happened and your best days are ahead. Make the most of each day, with this in mind that today will one day be the past so make it good TODAY. Lay regret aside!

- Insecurity; I am not good enough, not capable, inadequate, not the right candidate, feeling unworthy, being reminded of our short comings by society, our minds and our circumstances. They make us hide the one talent or the talents God has given us and are under-utilizing them because we don't operate at our fullest potential. Jesus came to fill those places of inadequacy with Himself, so that we can live this abundant life. Make peace with yourself that you are the only original of you with so much to give; regardless of whether somebody exceeds your talents in an area, that shouldn't discourage or disqualify you from being the best you. There's always someone better, always someone prettier, always someone smarter, always someone younger, stronger, wiser, bolder or more successful. Be the best you in Christ Jesus that God the Father created you to be! Your "YOU" is the BEST. Lay aside the weight!

- Distractions; This is a very slick weight because it is not blatantly obvious and it disguises itself under rational thinking, common sense, the obvious, keeping it real, television and social media, etc. I am not against these things, per se, but we have to be careful that we are not taking on unnecessary things that weigh on our minds or eat our time. When we sympathize with others for example, we must be careful to not make their problems our burdens, but in turn help them carry those things to God. They can serve as distractions on the mission. Pointless arguments and drama, proving points, bickering, etc. are time consuming endeavors we have to walk away from. People will talk ill of you even when you do good things and talk about you when you do bad; keep moving. Getting involved in drama, pointless chatter, vain conversations and philosophies (Col. 2v8) are distractions and time wasters that leave heaviness in our hearts (weights) without accomplishing anything positive. This is one of the enemy's timeless tactics to keep us from moving forward. Remember, "A stich in time saves nine." If we don't take care of it today, we will need more resources (time, energy, money, etc.) to fix the bigger problem later. The enemy uses distractions to accomplish that. BUT thank you Lord Jesus! You came to bring liberty, healing and vision in this area. Let us seize the day and the moment with zeal, boldness, joy and excellence.

THE SIN:

That sin, that thing needs to be laid down in order to move forward in abundant life. On the cross, it has no power and Jesus has overcome it. We are sanctified but also in the process of sanctification. Don't underestimate the power of sin's grip on an area of your life by calling it a weakness. In order to overcome an enemy you must identify it for what it is. When we call it a weakness, we numb our discernment sensors making it easier to carry that sin and make excuses for it.

When we get to that place in God where pleasing Him trumps everything else, that sin is laid down easily or faster. That doesn't mean perfection is complete, but it means the hold it has over us begins to diminish. We are taken glory to glory and faith to faith (2 Cor 3:18 and Rom 1:17).

What Jesus brings is righteousness, peace and joy in the Holy Ghost. We are no longer bound to sin. His finished work on the cross has made us more than conquerors over strongholds. Jesus brings new life, full of new beginnings, strength, hope and love. Yes it has a demanding cost, of a surrendered life in a bed of roses with some thorns still intact. It hurts to be saved at times, but God provides grace. But the bondage of slavery to sin is worse and Jesus always promised that even though He has a yoke (heavy price) for us to carry, it is lighter than that of darkness. The Christian walk and life is not problem proof, in fact the issues seem to flow at a faster pace, but we have the grace and power of Christ resting heavy on our lives to take us through the storms.

Jesus came to make Israel function in our lives in order, purpose, and passion. He came to teach us to be content in plenty or little, which is to have a great attitude in all circumstances. He came to show us that we don't have to be controlled by our feelings, emotions, intellect, or flesh. Rather, we can live in a place of praise, a life that glorifies God to the fullest, speaks the truth in love, fights for justice, operates in the wisdom of God, lives a healthy life, is successful and operates as the hands and feet of Jesus here on earth. AMEN!!

Conclusion/End Notes:

Roman 8v28: "And *we know that all things work together for the good to them that love God, to them who are the called according to his purpose."*

God used every detail in this story for his glory and the good of His people. He is God Almighty and is not thrown off by anything and nothing takes Him by surprise. He is the Ancient of Days and the all-wise God who has worked out every single detail in our lives. For Joseph, it may have seemed like it was over. His father thought it was over and his brothers were convinced it was over, but God was working it all out. It may seem impossible, out of this world, crazy and strange for the promise God has for your life. This is why he is working it out and not asking you to figure it out. It's time to enter His rest and let Him lead as the faithful shepherd that he is. Remember, this is His plan, His will and His assignment for your life. Trust Him in the mountains. Trust Him in the valleys. Trust Him in the night time and trust Him during the daylight. Trust Him in tears and in the joyful times.

The word He has spoken over your life and into you DNA will not return to Him void but accomplish that which God purposed it to do. Let your response to Jesus today be YES. Not only for salvation, but yes to go deeper into what he has for you. I'll emphasize again for the believer who has RELATIONSHIP (loves God and is the called) that ALL (everything, every failure, storm, trial, mishap, mix up, stupid move, success, idea, cheerful moment, sad situation, death, birth, rejection, humiliation, loss, gain, lack, surplus, child, marriage, divorce, setback) THINGS work (align themselves with a common purpose) for your good (benefit, joy, character development, perfection, shaping/molding). Let God work out all those details in your life and in the meantime, worship him by trusting him, rejoicing in him, staying faithful in him, loving him and people. He is working it all out and perfecting all concerns you. Let him do the impossible and you do the possible.

Hebrews 6v1; Therefore leaving the principles of the doctrines of Christ, let us go on unto perfection; not laying again the foundation of repentance from dead works, and of faith toward God.

We must always be excited about our salvation in Christ and being saved from eternal damnation in hell, but all the more aware that this is the beginning. When the deep of God calls to the depth in us, let us respond and allow all God called us to be, to manifest and give glory to God. After all, that depth is word spoken by God and it must come to pass as He intended. Jesus declared that we would do greater things. What does that greater look like concerning or involving you? What is your part in all this? Going another year without finding the answer to that question is unfair to you. (Habakkuk 2v2), *"Write down the vision and make it plain that he may run with it that readeth it."* What is your life's mission statement? What have you been placed here to accomplish? You have to give an account to God one day. So here are some helpful tips:

1. What games did you play as a child consistently and naturally? Children that played as doctors continuously usually end up as doctors (for example).
2. What dreams and visions did you think or talk about growing up? Currently what are your dreams and visions saying to you?
3. What did you do when no one was looking, in your leisure time? Pretended public speaking, drawing and art, preaching, braiding hair, designing clothes? All of those are indicators of what God has placed in you.
4. When you read the word of God, what stories or people, principles, etc., stand out to you the most? I wonder if mother Theresa was inspired by Dorcas, for example.
5. What are your gifts? I suggest spiritual gifts assessment tests that you can find online or through your local church family.
6. What bothers you in society that if you had the resources to fix it you would in a heartbeat?
7. What have parents, mentors, peers and enemies said about you? Joseph's brothers asked him if he would be ruler over them.
8. What and who are you drawn to?

9. How do you help in your local church?
10. What have sound prophets spoken over your life? Spoken, stirred up and prayed on?

In closing, I would like to share what the Joseph anointing looks like and has taught me. It is a very powerful anointing that brings change to millions of lives. The dream God has given you will change the lives of millions. Do not underestimate how powerful your dream is. Even if it blesses one person, that's incredible; you have no idea how they in turn will impact many other lives.

The Joseph anointing does the following:
1. Leaves a rich history of God in the earth and leaves a long lasting impact of change (Exodus 1v8). Well after he was gone, Joseph left an impact in Egypt, that other Pharaohs (except these two of Moses' time acknowledged him and allowed his people to flourish and multiply to great numbers in Egypt. It leaves a generational impact in this world.
2. Is a vision implementer; He is introduced to us as a big dreamer that the dungeon develops into a dream interpreter, then a vision caster into a vision implementer. This anointing is the change he or she longs to see and puts their faith and works into play to produce results. It carries out the vision with excellence, discipline, and Godly character.
3. Problem solvers: they are solutions to the crisis at hand or the one coming. They do not rest at the place of identifying the problem or crises only but would rather use and exercise the power and authority given to them to enrich the lives of others.
4. Natural born leaders that think out of the box and are severely allergic to mediocrity. They are a distinct breed of excellence, prospering in all that they do because anything done substandard goes against their character. They carry an aura of leadership and greatness (and the Lord was with him; he could be visibly seen on his life – Gen 39:3).
5. They are people God raises up in remembrance of His covenant with Abraham. He or she is raised to preserve the people of God (Israel and/or the remnant). Although the Joseph in you is incredibly gifted, the bigger picture is God allowed you to shine (flowing out of his kindness, favor and goodness) because He was honoring His word and faithfulness to Abraham (the covenant He made with him). You're a blessing to

Abraham's seed both natural and spiritual.

6. Operates in the spirit of excellence; when they work, they work well; they are talent multipliers and are guided by the laws of dominion, fruitfulness and multiplication. Subtraction and addition are used expertly and only when needed. Multiplication and fruitfulness are in their DNA.

7. Has a strong resemblance to Jesus Christ (the lion and the lamb). Very powerful, but extremely gentle and compassionate. This world renowned leader had the power to severely punish his accusers but moved in compassion and filled with meekness, he spared their lives and nourished them instead. Ultimately Joseph, like Jesus, had embraced the bigger picture of the Father's plan and design. Someone had to nail Jesus to the cross, someone had to betray him; likewise someone had to throw Joseph into a pit and sell him into slavery for a greater purpose. Sustaining God's people; which was done for the glory of God!

8. Walks in tremendous favor; it doesn't mean that their life doesn't have obstacles or that it is perfect; on the contrary as you see though the journey Joseph went through. Rather, they are noticeable in a crowd because of the aura and unique power and touch of God on their lives. They stand out very easily, but not always in the usual way others do. It is the depth of their speech, the fruitfulness of their actions and the excellence of their character. It shines. They glow. They are evidently different, strangely peculiar, and very loving people. One of the easiest ways to spot them, is that they hate being like everyone around them. Their positive outlook on life and their desire to operate in excellence is very strong. They are often asked or looked at with this in mind, "who are you?" "There's something different about you." Embrace this. Josephs always stand out and even in the oddest of places, God makes them shine.

9. They are a natural born leader, even though 11th in birth line, Joseph is an unusual leader. He's not your regular, cookie cut leader, but rather one constantly operating in the element of surprise. Joseph was a crazy dreamer and, unlike his brothers, very radical in thought and vison. He was a grand scale- type thinker and therefore, it makes sense that he received the first born leader award, also known as the double portion. He was 11th in line, but God made room for him to be awarded as first because of the unusual call and leadership anointing on his life. You may be last in line, but in the kingdom the last is first.

10. Has a supernatural attitude to embrace long suffering and allow the patience of God to keep them moving forward. What the average person (believer) would complain and murmur about doesn't seem to break them. There is a calmness of spirit about them, and a deep loyalty to Christ that even in the ugliest of times, they refuse to act out of character. It is the ability to encourage and lift up others when their own situation is not the best and maybe even worse than most in their sphere of influence. Joseph is able to glorify and honor God when Mrs. Potiphar approached him. He was able to minister to Pharaoh's chief baker and butler even though he was wrongfully placed in the dungeon. Bitterness is not this anointing's portion. The dream is too big to give up before it is birthed.

11. It has a global impact; this may discourage some and make you feel that this book isn't for you. Hold on, before you totally disregard me. I believe, as I stated earlier, that there is a Joseph in all of us as we all have a dream, purpose and destiny. For some, it is on larger scales and some smaller. All that is up to God the Father, but we all have a Joseph in us. This, however, is the one called to impact nations on a scale that Joseph did. So, if you have disregarded the size of your dreams, revisit them. This is no small calling.

12. Has an absolute love for family; they carry responsibility to help advance their family, biological or divine, with the assignment to nourish them with the best. His people lived in Goshen (the best of the land) tending to Pharaoh's herds, plus theirs (with the best in the industry) and they were blossoming in life as God's people, the seed of Abraham (as the best of lifestyles). A love of present family and family to come. A belief in the power of a rich legacy, and passing on the baton from generation to generation.

13. Walks in dominion; he ruled and excelled in his father's house, ruled in the dungeon and ruled over Egypt. It's not just about being a leader, Joseph had dominion in leadership. God intended for us to live at this capacity and gave us Eden as the birthing place for this, to ripple effect into all the earth. This anointing exercises authority by heavenly command. No matter where they are they blossom in greatness.

14. Has great discipline and obedience; an individual who with great power will exercise his or her dominion, but clearly set within boundaries. There are clear examples of this in Joseph's life (respect for his father, respect

for Potiphar, respect for the jailor and respect for Pharaoh), but the one that fascinates me the most is this; Joseph is now the most powerful man in the world, but doesn't go out seeking his father. I believe God forbade him and told him to stay put in Egypt and He would bring him full circle. Joseph, by now, had forgiven his brothers. If he hadn't, this story would have ended a whole new way. He has skilled warriors at his disposal to attack his brothers if he desired to seek after his father, should they threaten his life again. Why wouldn't he go back to Canaan and in search of Jacob? Was he afraid to find his father deceased and suffer the wrath of his brothers? Was he afraid of how he'd use his power to punish his brothers? I don't know, but what I do know is Joseph was so extremely disciplined and obedient to leadership of the Lord in his life, that he kept his peace and remained in Egypt. In fact, the only time he returned to Canaan (alive) was to bury his father Jacob. Hundreds of years later, his bones were carried back to Canaan to be buried when the children of Israel took the great Exodus to the Promised Land.

I hope you reading this book has blessed you as much (and even more) as it did me to write it. I pray that your dreams do come true and that you live the abundant life Jesus died for you to have. I speak a blessing over you and protection by the blood of Jesus that you will have dominion in all that your hands and mind are set to do for the glory of God. My prayer is that you will hold your head up higher knowing that God has a special purpose for you and it's not too late to be all God purposed you to be. Dream the dreams God has for you, pursue them and, LIVE free in the dreamer's anointing that rests heavy on your life. *But let patience have her perfect work, that ye may be perfect and entire, wanting nothing (James 1:4,* as God forms you daily into spiritual Israel. Put your Jacob on his death bed and let him speak to the Israel in you. Only when Jacob dies [as one dies to self] will Israel flourish to the wonder he is; the wonder you are. SHALOM!

Made in the USA
Lexington, KY
12 May 2018